THE POSY RING

THE POSY RING

A BOOK OF VERSE FOR CHILDREN

CHOSEN AND CLASSIFIED BY

Kate Douglas Wiggin

AND

Nora Archibald Smith

*"A box of jewels, shop of rarities,
A ring whose posy was 'My pleasure'"*
GEORGE HERBERT

Granger Index Reprint Series

 BOOKS FOR LIBRARIES PRESS
FREEPORT, NEW YORK

First Published 1903
Reprinted 1970

STANDARD BOOK NUMBER:
8369-6193-5

LIBRARY OF CONGRESS CATALOG CARD NUMBER:
70-128164

68,969

PUBLIC NOTICE.—*This is to state,*
That these are the specimens left at the gate
Of Pinafore Palace, exact to date,
In the hands of the porter, Curlypate,
Who sits in his plush on a chair of state,
By somebody who is a candidate
For the office of Lilliput Laureate.
                    William Brighty Rands.

CONTENTS

	Page
LILLIPUT NOTICE. By *William Brighty Rands*	IX

A YEAR'S WINDFALLS

Marjorie's Almanac. By *Thomas Bailey Aldrich*	3
In February. By *John Addington Symonds*	5
March. By *William Wordsworth*	6
Nearly Ready. By *Mary Mapes Dodge*	7
Spring Song. By *George Eliot*	7
In April. By *Elizabeth Akers*	8
Spring. By *Celia Thaxter*	9
The Voice of Spring. By *Mary Howitt*	10
The Coming of Spring. By *Nora Perry*	11
May. By *Frank Dempster Sherman*	13
Spring and Summer. By "*A.*"	14
Summer Days. By *Christina G. Rossetti*	15
September. By *H. H.*	16
How the Leaves Came Down. By *Susan Coolidge*	17
Winter Night. By *Mary F. Butts*	19
A Year's Windfalls. By *Christina G. Rossetti*	20

CONTENTS

THE CHILD'S WORLD

	Page
The Wonderful World. By *William Brighty Rands*	27
A Day. By *Emily Dickinson*	28
Good-Morning. By *Robert Browning*	29
What the Winds Bring. By *Edmund Clarence Stedman*	29
Lady Moon. By *Lord Houghton*	30
O Lady Moon. By *Christina G. Rossetti*	31
Windy Nights. By *Robert Louis Stevenson*	31
Wild Winds. By *Mary F. Butts*	32
Now the Noisy Winds are Still. By *Mary Mapes Dodge*	33
The Wind. *Letitia E. Landon*	33
The Fountain. By *James Russell Lowell*	34
The Waterfall. By *Frank Dempster Sherman*	35
The Voice of the Grass. By *Sarah Roberts Boyle*	36
The Wind in a Frolic. By *William Howitt*	38
Clouds. By *Frank Dempster Sherman*	40
Signs of Rain. By *Edward Jenner*	41
A Sudden Shower. By *James Whitcomb Riley*	43
Strange Lands By *Laurence Alma Tadema*	44
Guessing Song. By *Henry Johnstone*	45
The Rivulet. By *Lucy Larcom*	46
Jack Frost. By *Hannah F. Gould*	47
Snowflakes. By *Mary Mapes Dodge*	49
The Water! The Water. By *William Motherwell*	49

CONTENTS

HIAWATHA'S CHICKENS

	Page
The Swallows. By *Edwin Arnold*	53
The Swallow's Nest. By *Edwin Arnold*	53
The Birds in Spring. By *Thomas Nashe*	54
Robin Redbreast. By *William Allingham*	54
The Lark and the Rook. *Unknown*	56
The Snowbird. By *Hezekiah Butterworth*	57
Who Stole the Bird's Nest? By *Lydia Maria Child*	59
Answer to a Child's Question. By *Samuel Taylor Coleridge*	62
The Burial of the Linnet. By *Juliana H. Ewing*	63
The Titmouse. By *Ralph Waldo Emerson*	64
Birds in Summer. By *Mary Howitt*	65
An Epitaph on a Robin Redbreast. By *Samuel Rogers*	67
The Bluebird. By *Emily Huntington Miller*	68
Song. By *John Keats*	69
What Does Little Birdie Say? By *Alfred, Lord Tennyson*	69
The Owl. By *Alfred, Lord Tennyson*	70
Wild Geese. By *Celia Thaxter*	71
Chanticleer. By *Celia Thaxter*	72
The Singer. By *Edmund Clarence Stedman*	73
The Blue Jay. By *Susan Hartley Swett*	74
Robert of Lincoln. By *William Cullen Bryant*	75

CONTENTS

HIAWATHA'S CHICKENS—*Continued*

	Page
White Butterflies. By *Algernon C. Swinburne*	78
The Ant and the Cricket. *Unknown*	78

THE FLOWER FOLK

Little White Lily. By *George Macdonald*	83
Violets. By *Dinah Maria Mulock*	85
Young Dandelion. By *Dinah Maria Mulock*	86
Baby Seed Song. By *E. Nesbit*	88
A Violet Bank. By *William Shakespeare*	88
There's Nothing Like the Rose. By *Christina G. Rossetti*	89
Snowdrops. By *Laurence Alma Tadema*	89
Fern Song. By *John B. Tabb*	90
The Violet. By *Jane Taylor*	90
Daffy-Down-Dilly. By *Anna B. Warner*	91
Baby Corn. *Unknown*	93
A Child's Fancy. By "*A.*"	95
Little Dandelion. By *Helen B. Bostwick*	97
Dandelions. By *Helen Gray Cone*	98
The Flax Flower. By *Mary Howitt*	99
Dear Little Violets. By *John Moultrie*	101
Child's Song in Spring. By *E. Nesbit*	102
The Tree. By *Björnstjerne Bjoörnson*	102
The Daisy's Song. By *John Keats*	103
Song. By *Thomas Love Peacock*	104
For Good Luck. By *Juliana Horatia Ewing*	105

CONTENTS

HIAWATHA'S BROTHERS

	Page
My Pony. By "*A*."	109
On a Spaniel, Called Beau, Killing a Young Bird. By *William Cowper*	111
Beau's Reply. By *William Cowper*	112
Seal Lullaby. By *Rudyard Kipling*	113
Milking Time. By *Christina G. Rossetti*	113
Thank You, Pretty Cow. By *Jane Taylor*	114
The Boy and the Sheep. By *Ann Taylor*	114
Lambs in the Meadow. By *Laurence Alma Tadema*	115
The Pet Lamb. By *William Wordsworth*	116
The Kitten, and Falling Leaves. By *William Wordsworth*	121

OTHER LITTLE CHILDREN

Where Go the Boats? By *Robert Louis Stevenson*	125
Cleanliness. By *Charles and Mary Lamb*	126
Wishing. By *William Allingham*	127
The Boy. By *William Allingham*	128
Infant Joy. By *William Blake*	129
A Blessing for the Blessed. By *Laurence Alma Tadema*	129
Piping Down the Valleys Wild. By *William Blake*	131
A Sleeping Child. By *Arthur Hugh Clough*	132
Birdies with Broken Wings. By *Mary Mapes Dodge*	133

CONTENTS

OTHER LITTLE CHILDREN—*Continued*

	Page
Seven Times One. By *Jean Ingelow*	133
I Remember, I Remember. By *Thomas Hood*	135
Good-Night and Good-Morning. By *Lord Houghton*	136
Little Children. By *Mary Howitt*	137
The Angel's Whisper. By *Samuel Lover*	139
Little Garaine. By *Sir Gilbert Parker*	140
A Letter. By *Matthew Prior*	141
Love and the Child. By *William Brighty Rands*	142
Polly. By *William Brighty Rands*	143
A Chill. By *Christina G. Rossetti*	144
A Child's Laughter. By *Algernon C. Swinburne*	145
The World's Music. By *Gabriel Setoun*	146
The Little Land. By *Robert Louis Stevenson*	148
In a Garden. By *Algernon C. Swinburne*	151
Little Gustava. By *Celia Thaxter*	152
A Bunch of Roses. By *John B. Tabb*	155
The Child at Bethlehem. By *John B. Tabb*	155
After the Storm. By *W. M. Thackeray*	156
Lucy Gray. By *William Wordsworth*	156
Deaf and Dumb. By "*A.*"	159
The Blind Boy. By *Colley Cibber*	160

PLAY-TIME

A Boy's Song. By *James Hogg*	165
The Lost Doll. By *Charles Kingsley*	166

CONTENTS

PLAY-TIME—*Continued*

	Page
Dolladine. By *William Brighty Rands*	167
Dressing the Doll. By *William Brighty Rands*	167
The Pedlar's Caravan. By *William Brighty Rands*	170
A Sea-Song from the Shore. *James Whitcomb Riley*	171
The Land of Story-Books. By *Robert Louis Stevenson*	172
The City Child. By *Alfred, Lord Tennyson*	173
Going into Breeches. By *Charles and Mary Lamb*	174
Hunting Song. By *Samuel Taylor Coleridge*	176
Hie Away. By *Sir Walter Scott*	176

STORY TIME

The Fairy Folk. By *Robert Bird*	181
A Fairy in Armor. By *Joseph Rodman Drake*	183
The Last Voyage of the Fairies. By *W. H. Davenport Adams*	184
A New Fern. By "*A.*"	186
The Child and the Fairies. By "*A.*"	187
The Little Elf. By *John Kendrick Bangs*	188
"One, Two, Three." By *Henry C. Bunner*	188
What May Happen to a Thimble. By "*B.*"	190
Discontent. By *Sarah Orne Jewett*	193
The Nightingale and the Glowworm. By *William Cowper*	195
Thanksgiving Day. By *Lydia Maria Child*	196

CONTENTS

STORY TIME—*Continued*

	Page
A Thanksgiving Fable. By *Oliver Herford*	197
The Magpie's Nest. By *Charles and Mary Lamb*	198
The Owl and the Pussy-Cat. By *Edward Lear*	201
A Lobster Quadrille. By *Lewis Carroll*	202
The Fairies' Shopping. By *Margaret Deland*	204
Fable. By *Ralph Waldo Emerson*	206
A Midsummer Song. By *Richard Watson Gilder*	207
The Fairies of the Caldon-Low. By *Mary Howitt*	209
The Elf and the Dormouse. By *Oliver Herford*	213
Meg Merrilies. By *John Keats*	214
Romance. By *Gabriel Setoun*	215
The Cow-Boy's Song. By *Anna M. Wells*	217

BED TIME

Auld Daddy Darkness. By *James Ferguson*	221
Wynken, Blynken, and Nod. By *Eugene Field*	222
Rockaby, Lullaby. By *Josiah Gilbert Holland*	224
Sleep, My Treasure. By *E. Nesbit*	225
Lullaby of an Infant Chief. By *Sir Walter Scott*	226
Sweet and Low. By *Alfred, Lord Tennyson*	227
Old Gaelic Lullaby. *Unknown*	228
The Sandman. By *Margaret Vandegrift*	228
The Cottager to Her Infant. By *Dorothy Wordsworth*	230
A Charm to Call Sleep. By *Henry Johnstone*	231
Night. By *Mary F. Butts*	232

CONTENTS xix

BED TIME—*Continued*

	Page
Bed-Time. By *Lord Rosslyn*	232
Nightfall in Dordrecht. By *Eugene Field*	233

FOR SUNDAY'S CHILD

All Things Bright and Beautiful. By *Cecil F. Alexander*	237
The Still Small Voice. By *Alexander Smart*	238
The Camel's Nose. By *Lydia H. Sigourney*	240
A Child's Grace. By *Robert Burns*	241
A Child's Thought of God. By *Elizabeth B. Browning*	241
The Lamb. By *William Blake*	242
Night and Day. By *Mary Mapes Dodge*	243
High and Low. By *Dora Read Goodale*	244
By Cool Siloam's Shady Rill. By *Reginald Heber*	244
Sheep and Lambs. By *Katharine Tynan Hinkson*	245
To His Saviour, a Child; A Present by a Child. By *Robert Herrick*	246
What Would You See? By George Macdonald	247
Corn-Fields. By *Mary Howitt*	248
Little Christel. By *William Brighty Rands*	250
A Child's Prayer. By *M. Betham Edwards*	252

BELLS OF CHRISTMAS

The Adoration of the Wise Men. By *Cecil F. Alexander*	257
Cradle Hymn. By *Isaac Watts*	258

CONTENTS

BELLS OF CHRISTMAS—*Continued*

	Page
The Christmas Silence. By *Margaret Deland*	260
An Offertory. By *Mary Mapes Dodge*	261
Why Do Bells of Christmas Ring? By *Eugene Field*	261
A Visit from St. Nicholas. By *Clement C. Moore*	262
The Christmas Trees. By *Mary F. Butts*	265
A Birthday Gift. By *Christina G. Rossetti*	267
A Christmas Lullaby. By *John Addington Symonds*	267
I Saw Three Ships. *Old Carol*	268
Santa Claus. *Unknown*	269
Neighbors of the Christ Night. By *Nora Archibald Smith*	271
Cradle Hymn. By *Martin Luther*	272
The Christmas Holly. By *Eliza Cook*	273
LILLIPUT NOTICE. By *William Brighty Rands*	274

THE POSY RING

I

A YEAR'S WINDFALLS

Who comes dancing over the snow,
  His soft little feet all bare and rosy?
Open the door, though the wild winds blow,
  Take the child in and make him cosy.
  Take him in and hold him dear,
  He is the wonderful glad New Year.

  Dinah M. Mulock.

A YEAR'S WINDFALLS

Marjorie's Almanac

Robins in the tree-top,
  Blossoms in the grass,
Green things a-growing
  Everywhere you pass;
Sudden little breezes,
  Showers of silver dew,
Black bough and bent twig
  Budding out anew;
Pine-tree and willow-tree,
  Fringèd elm and larch,—
Don't you think that May-time's
  Pleasanter than March?

Apples in the orchard
  Mellowing one by one;
Strawberries upturning
  Soft cheeks to the sun;
Roses faint with sweetness,
  Lilies fair of face,
Drowsy scents and murmurs
  Haunting every place;

THE POSY RING

Lengths of golden sunshine,
  Moonlight bright as day,—
Don't you think that summer's
  Pleasanter than May?

Roger in the corn-patch
  Whistling negro songs;
Pussy by the hearth-side
  Romping with the tongs;
Chestnuts in the ashes
  Bursting through the rind;
Red leaf and gold leaf
  Rustling down the wind;
Mother "doin' peaches"
  All the afternoon,—
Don't you think that autumn's
  Pleasanter than June?

Little fairy snow-flakes
  Dancing in the flue;
Old Mr. Santa Claus,
  What is keeping you?
Twilight and firelight
  Shadows come and go;
Merry chime of sleigh-bells
  Tinkling through the snow;
Mother knitting stockings
  (Pussy's got the ball),—

THE POSY RING

Don't you think that winter's
  Pleasanter than all?

    Thomas Bailey Aldrich.

In February

The birds have been singing to-day,
  And saying: "The spring is near!
The sun is as warm as in May,
  And the deep blue heavens are clear."

The little bird on the boughs
  Of the sombre snow-laden pine
Thinks: "Where shall I build me my house,
  And how shall I make it fine?

"For the season of snow is past;
  The mild south wind is on high;
And the scent of the spring is cast
  From his wing as he hurries by."

The little birds twitter and cheep
  To their loves on the leafless larch;
But seven feet deep the snow-wreaths sleep,
  And the year hath not worn to March.

    John Addington Symonds.

THE POSY RING

March

The cock is crowing,
The stream is flowing,
The small birds twitter,
The lake doth glitter,
The green field sleeps in the sun;
  The oldest and youngest
  Are at work with the strongest;
  The cattle are grazing,
  Their heads never raising;
There are forty feeding like one.

  Like an army defeated
  The snow hath retreated,
  And now doth fare ill
  On the top of the bare hill;
The ploughboy is whooping—anon—anon!
  There's joy on the mountains;
  There's life in the fountains;
  Small clouds are sailing,
  Blue sky prevailing;
The rain is over and gone.

William Wordsworth.

THE POSY RING

Nearly Ready

In the snowing and the blowing,
   In the cruel sleet,
Little flowers begin their growing
   Far beneath our feet.
Softly taps the Spring, and cheerly,
   "Darlings, are you here?"
Till they answer, "We are nearly,
   Nearly ready, dear."

"Where is Winter, with his snowing?
   Tell us, Spring," they say.
Then she answers, "He is going,
   Going on his way.
Poor old Winter does not love you;
   But his time is past;
Soon my birds shall sing above you,—
   Set you free at last."

Mary Mapes Dodge.

Spring Song

Spring comes hither,
   Buds the rose;
Roses wither,
   Sweet spring goes.

Summer soars,—
  Wide-winged day;
White light pours,
  Flies away.

Soft winds blow,
  Westward born;
Onward go,
  Toward the morn.
                        George Eliot.

In April

The poplar drops beside the way
Its tasselled plumes of silver-gray;
The chestnut pouts its great brown buds
Impatient for the laggard May.

The honeysuckles lace the wall,
The hyacinths grow fair and tall;
And mellow sun and pleasant wind
And odorous bees are over all.
                        Elizabeth Akers.

THE POSY RING

Spring

The alder by the river
  Shakes out her powdery curls;
The willow buds in silver
  For little boys and girls.

The little birds fly over,
  And oh, how sweet they sing!
To tell the happy children
  That once again 'tis spring.

The gay green grass comes creeping
  So soft beneath their feet;
The frogs begin to ripple
  A music clear and sweet.

And buttercups are coming,
  And scarlet columbine;
And in the sunny meadows
  The dandelions shine.

And just as many daisies
  As their soft hands can hold
The little ones may gather,
  All fair in white and gold.

Here blows the warm red clover,
  There peeps the violet blue;
O happy little children,
  God made them all for you!
                    Celia Thaxter.

The Voice of Spring

I am coming, I am coming!
Hark! the little bee is humming;
See, the lark is soaring high
In the blue and sunny sky;
And the gnats are on the wing,
Wheeling round in airy ring.

See, the yellow catkins cover
All the slender willows over!
And on the banks of mossy green
Star-like primroses are seen;
And, their clustering leaves below,
White and purple violets blow.

Hark! the new-born lambs are bleating,
And the cawing rooks are meeting
In the elms,—a noisy crowd;
All the birds are singing loud;
And the first white butterfly
In the sunshine dances by.

Look around thee, look around!
Flowers in all the fields abound;
Every running stream is bright;
All the orchard trees are white;
And each small and waving shoot
Promises sweet flowers and fruit.

THE POSY RING

Turn thine eyes to earth and heaven:
God for thee the spring has given,
Taught the birds their melodies,
Clothed the earth, and cleared the skies,
For thy pleasure or thy food:
Pour thy soul in gratitude.

Mary Howitt.

The Coming of Spring

There's something in the air
That's new and sweet and rare—
A scent of summer things,
A whir as if of wings.

There's something, too, that's new
In the color of the blue
That's in the morning sky,
Before the sun is high.

And though on plain and hill
'Tis winter, winter still,
There's something seems to say
That winter's had its day.

And all this changing tint,
This whispering stir and hint
Of bud and bloom and wing,
Is the coming of the spring.

And to-morrow or to-day
The brooks will break away
From their icy, frozen sleep,
And run, and laugh, and leap.

And the next thing, in the woods,
The catkins in their hoods
Of fur and silk will stand,
A sturdy little band.

And the tassels soft and fine
Of the hazel will entwine,
And the elder branches show
Their buds against the snow.

So, silently but swift,
Above the wintry drift,
The long days gain and gain,
Until on hill and plain,—

Once more, and yet once more,
Returning as before,
We see the bloom of birth
Make young again the earth.

      Nora Perry.

THE POSY RING

May

May shall make the world anew;
Golden sun and silver dew,
Money minted in the sky,
Shall the earth's new garments buy.
May shall make the orchards bloom;
And the blossoms' fine perfume
Shall set all the honey-bees
Murmuring among the trees.
May shall make the bud appear
Like a jewel, crystal clear,
'Mid the leaves upon the limb
Where the robin lilts his hymn.
May shall make the wild flowers tell
Where the shining snowflakes fell;
Just as though each snow-flake's heart,
By some secret, magic art,
Were transmuted to a flower
In the sunlight and the shower.
Is there such another, pray,
Wonder-making month as May?

     Frank Dempster Sherman.

Spring and Summer

Spring is growing up,
  Is not it a pity?
She was such a little thing,
  And so very pretty!
Summer is extremely grand,
  We must pay her duty,
(But it is to little Spring
  That she owes her beauty!)

All the buds are blown,
  Trees are dark and shady,
(It was Spring who dress'd them, though,
  Such a little lady!)
And the birds sing loud and sweet
  Their enchanting hist'ries,
(It was Spring who taught them, though,
  Such a singing mistress!)

From the glowing sky
  Summer shines above us;
Spring was such a little dear,
  But will Summer love us?
She is very beautiful,
  With her grown-up blisses,
Summer we must bow before;
  Spring we coaxed with kisses!

THE POSY RING

Spring is growing up,
  Leaving us so lonely,
In the place of little Spring
  We have Summer only!
Summer with her lofty airs,
  And her stately faces,
In the place of little Spring,
  With her childish graces!

"A."

Summer Days

Winter is cold-hearted;
  Spring is yea and nay;
Autumn is a weathercock,
  Blown every way:
Summer days for me,
When every leaf is on its tree,

When Robin's not a beggar,
  And Jenny Wren's a bride,
And larks hang, singing, singing, singing,
  Over the wheat-fields wide,
  And anchored lilies ride,
And the pendulum spider
  Swings from side to side,

And blue-black beetles transact business,
  And gnats fly in a host,

And furry caterpillars hasten
  That no time be lost,
And moths grow fat and thrive,
And ladybirds arrive.

Before green apples blush,
  Before green nuts embrown,
Why, one day in the country
  Is worth a month in town—
  Is worth a day and a year
Of the dusty, musty, lag-last fashion
  That days drone elsewhere.
                    Christina G. Rossetti.

September

The goldenrod is yellow,
  The corn is turning brown,
The trees in apple orchards
  With fruit are bending down;

The gentian's bluest fringes
  Are curling in the sun;
In dusty pods the milkweed
  Its hidden silk has spun;

The sedges flaunt their harvest
  In every meadow nook,
And asters by the brookside
  Make asters in the brook;

THE POSY RING

From dewy lanes at morning
  The grapes' sweet odors rise;
At noon the roads all flutter
  With yellow butterflies—

By all these lovely tokens
  September days are here,
With summer's best of weather
  And autumn's best of cheer.

H. H.

How the Leaves Came Down

I'll tell you how the leaves came down.
  The great Tree to his children said,
"You're getting sleepy, Yellow and Brown,
  Yes, very sleepy, little Red;
  It is quite time you went to bed."

"Ah!" begged each silly, pouting leaf,
  "Let us a little longer stay;
Dear Father Tree, behold our grief,
  'Tis such a very pleasant day
  We do not want to go away."

So, just for one more merry day
  To the great Tree the leaflets clung,
Frolicked and danced and had their way,
  Upon the autumn breezes swung,
  Whispering all their sports among,

"Perhaps the great Tree will forget
  And let us stay until the spring,
If we all beg and coax and fret."
  But the great Tree did no such thing;
  He smiled to hear their whispering.

"Come, children all, to bed," he cried;
  And ere the leaves could urge their prayer
He shook his head, and far and wide,
  Fluttering and rustling everywhere,
  Down sped the leaflets through the air.

I saw them; on the ground they lay,
  Golden and red, a huddled swarm,
Waiting till one from far away,
  White bed-clothes heaped upon her arm,
  Should come to wrap them safe and warm.

The great bare Tree looked down and smiled.
  "Good-night, dear little leaves," he said;
And from below each sleepy child
  Replied "Good-night," and murmured,
  "It is *so* nice to go to bed."

Susan Coolidge.

Winter Night

Blow, wind, blow!
Drift the flying snow!
Send it twirling, whirling overhead!
    There's a bedroom in a tree
    Where, snug as snug can be,
The squirrel nests in his cosey bed.

Shriek, wind, shriek!
Make the branches creak!
Battle with the boughs till break o' day!
    In a snow-cave warm and tight,
    Through the icy winter night
The rabbit sleeps the peaceful hours away.

Call, wind, call,
In entry and in hall,
Straight from off the mountain white and wild!
    Soft purrs the pussy-cat
    On her little fluffy mat,
And beside her nestles close her furry child.

Scold, wind, scold,
So bitter and so bold!
Shake the windows with your tap, tap, tap!
    With half-shut, dreamy eyes
    The drowsy baby lies
Cuddled closely in his mother's lap.

                      Mary F. Butts.

A Year's Windfalls

On the wind of January
  Down flits the snow,
Travelling from the frozen North
  As cold as it can blow.
Poor robin redbreast,
  Look where he comes;
Let him in to feel your fire,
  And toss him of your crumbs.

On the wind in February
  Snowflakes float still,
Half inclined to turn to rain,
  Nipping, dripping, chill.
Then the thaws swell the streams,
  And swollen rivers swell the sea:—
If the winter ever ends
  How pleasant it will be.

In the wind of windy March
  The catkins drop down,
Curly, caterpillar-like,
  Curious green and brown.
With concourse of nest-building birds
  And leaf-buds by the way,
We begin to think of flowers
  And life and nuts some day.

THE POSY RING

With the gusts of April
  Rich fruit-tree blossoms fall,
On the hedged-in orchard-green,
  From the southern wall.
Apple-trees and pear-trees
  Shed petals white or pink,
Plum-trees and peach-trees;
  While sharp showers sink and sink.

Little brings the May breeze
  Beside pure scent of flowers,
While all things wax and nothing wanes
  In lengthening daylight hours.
Across the hyacinth beds
  The wind lags warm and sweet,
Across the hawthorn tops,
  Across the blades of wheat.

In the wind of sunny June
  Thrives the red rose crop,
Every day fresh blossoms blow
  While the first leaves drop;
White rose and yellow rose
  And moss rose choice to find,
And the cottage cabbage-rose
  Not one whit behind.

On the blast of scorched July
  Drives the pelting hail,

From thunderous lightning-clouds, that blot
   Blue heaven grown lurid-pale.
Weedy waves are tossed ashore,
   Sea-things strange to sight
Gasp upon the barren shore
   And fade away in light.

In the parching August wind
   Corn-fields bow the head,
Sheltered in round valley depths,
   On low hills outspread.
Early leaves drop loitering down
   Weightless on the breeze,
First fruits of the year's decay
   From the withering trees.

In brisk wind of September
   The heavy-headed fruits
Shake upon their bending boughs
   And drop from the shoots;
Some glow golden in the sun,
   Some show green and streaked,
Some set forth a purple bloom,
   Some blush rosy-cheeked.

In strong blast of October
   At the equinox,
Stirred up in his hollow bed
   Broad ocean rocks;

THE POSY RING

Plunge the ships on his bosom,
  Leaps and plunges the foam,
It's oh! for mothers' sons at sea,
  That they were safe at home.

In slack wind of November
  The fog forms and shifts;
All the world comes out again
  When the fog lifts.
Loosened from their sapless twigs
  Leaves drop with every gust;
Drifting, rustling, out of sight
  In the damp or dust.

Last of all, December,
  The year's sands nearly run,
Speeds on the shortest day,
  Curtails the sun;
With its bleak raw wind
  Lays the last leaves low,
Brings back the nightly frosts,
  Brings back the snow.

Christina G. Rossetti.

II

THE CHILD'S WORLD

Great, wide, beautiful, wonderful World,
With the wonderful water round you curled,
And the wonderful grass upon your breast,
World, you are beautifully drest.
William Brighty Rands.

THE CHILD'S WORLD

The Wonderful World

Great, wide, beautiful, wonderful World,
With the wonderful water round you curled,
And the wonderful grass upon your breast,
World, you are beautifully drest.

The wonderful air is over me,
And the wonderful wind is shaking the tree—
It walks on the water, and whirls the mills,
And talks to itself on the top of the hills.

You friendly Earth, how far do you go,
With the wheat-fields that nod and the rivers
    that flow,
With cities and gardens, and cliffs and isles,
And people upon you for thousands of miles?

Ah! you are so great, and I am so small,
I hardly can think of you, World, at all;
And yet, when I said my prayers to-day,
My mother kissed me, and said, quite gay,

"If the wonderful World is great to you,
And great to father and mother, too,
You are more than the Earth, though you are such a dot!
You can love and think, and the Earth cannot!"
William Brighty Rands.

A Day

I'll tell you how the sun rose,
A ribbon at a time.
The steeples swam in amethyst,
The news like squirrels ran.

The hills untied their bonnets,
The bobolinks begun.
Then I said softly to myself,
"That must have been the sun!"

. . . .

But how he set, I know not.
There seemed a purple stile
Which little yellow boys and girls
Were climbing all the while

Till when they reached the other side,
A dominie in gray
Put gently up the evening bars,
And led the flock away.
Emily Dickinson.

THE POSY RING

Good-Morning

The year's at the Spring,
And day's at the morn;
Morning's at seven;
The hill-side's dew-pearled;
The lark's on the wing;
The snail's on the thorn;
God's in his heaven—
All's right with the world.

     Robert Browning.

What the Winds Bring

Which is the Wind that brings the cold?
 The North-Wind, Freddy, and all the snow;
And the sheep will scamper into the fold
 When the North begins to blow.

Which is the Wind that brings the heat?
 The South-Wind, Katy; and corn will grow,
And peaches redden for you to eat,
 When the South begins to blow.

Which is the Wind that brings the rain?
 The East-Wind, Arty; and farmers know
The cows come shivering up the lane,
 When the East begins to blow.

Which is the Wind that brings the flowers?
   The West-Wind, Bessy; and soft and low
The birdies sing in the summer hours,
   When the West begins to blow.

                    Edmund Clarence Stedman.

Lady Moon

Lady Moon, Lady Moon, where are you roving?
   "Over the sea."
Lady Moon, Lady Moon, whom are you loving?
   "All that love me."

Are you not tired with rolling, and never
   Resting to sleep?
Why look so pale and so sad, as forever
   Wishing to weep?

"Ask me not this, little child, if you love me:
   You are too bold:
I must obey my dear Father above me,
   And do as I'm told."

Lady Moon, Lady Moon, where are you roving?
   "Over the sea."
Lady Moon, Lady Moon, whom are you loving?
   "All that love me."

                           Lord Houghton

O Lady Moon

O Lady Moon, your horns point toward the east:
    Shine, be increased;
O Lady Moon, your horns point toward the west:
    Wane, be at rest.

                Christina G. Rossetti.

Windy Nights

Whenever the moon and stars are set,
    Whenever the wind is high,
All night long in the dark and wet,
    A man goes riding by,
Late at night when the fires are out,
Why does he gallop and gallop about?

Whenever the trees are crying aloud,
    And ships are tossed at sea,
By, on the highway, low and loud,
    By at the gallop goes he.
By at the gallop he goes, and then
By he comes back at the gallop again.

                Robert Louis Stevenson.

Wild Winds

Oh, oh, how the wild winds blow!
      Blow high,
      Blow low,
    And whirlwinds go,
To chase the little leaves that fly—
    Fly low and high,
To hollow and to steep hill-side;
They shiver in the dreary weather,
And creep in little heaps together,
And nestle close and try to hide.

Oh, oh, how the wild winds blow!
      Blow low,
      Blow high,
    And whirlwinds try
To find a crevice—to find a crack,
They whirl to the front; they whirl to the back.
But Tommy and Will and the baby together
Are snug and safe from the wintry weather.
    All the winds that blow
    Cannot touch a toe—
    Cannot twist or twirl
    One silken curl.
They may rattle the doors in a noisy pack,
But the blazing fires will drive them back.

                            Mary F. Butts.

THE POSY RING

Now the Noisy Winds Are Still

Now the noisy winds are still;
April's coming up the hill!
All the spring is in her train,
Led by shining ranks of rain;
    Pit, pat, patter, clatter,
      Sudden sun, and clatter, patter!—
First the blue, and then the shower;
Bursting bud, and smiling flower;
Brooks set free with tinkling ring;
Birds too full of song to sing;
Crisp old leaves astir with pride,
Where the timid violets hide,—
All things ready with a will,—
April's coming up the hill!

              Mary Mapes Dodge.

The Wind

The wind has a language, I would I could learn;
Sometimes 'tis soothing, and sometimes 'tis stern;
Sometimes it comes like a low, sweet song,
And all things grow calm, as the sound floats along;
And the forest is lulled by the dreamy strain;
And slumber sinks down on the wandering main;

And its crystal arms are folded in rest,
And the tall ship sleeps on its heaving breast.

                Letitia Elizabeth Landon.

The Fountain

Into the sunshine,
  Full of the light,
Leaping and flashing
  From morn till night!

Into the moonlight,
  Whiter than snow,
Waving so flower-like
  When the winds blow!

Into the starlight,
  Rushing in spray,
Happy at midnight,
  Happy by day;

Ever in motion,
  Blithesome and cheery,
Still climbing heavenward,
  Never aweary;

Glad of all weathers;
  Still seeming best,
Upward or downward;
  Motion thy rest;

Full of a nature
  Nothing can tame,
Changed every moment,
  Ever the same;

Ceaseless aspiring,
  Ceaseless content,
Darkness or sunshine
  Thy element;

Glorious fountain!
  Let my heart be
Fresh, changeful, constant,
  Upward like thee!

         James Russell Lowell.

The Waterfall

Tinkle, tinkle!
Listen well!
Like a fairy silver bell
In the distance ringing,
Lightly swinging
In the air;
'Tis the water in the dell
Where the elfin minstrels dwell,
Falling in a rainbow sprinkle,
Dropping stars that brightly twinkle,
Bright and fair,

On the darkling pool below,
Making music so;
'Tis the water elves who play
On their lutes of spray.
Tinkle, tinkle!
Like a fairy silver bell;
Like a pebble in a shell;
Tinkle, tinkle!
Listen well!

    Frank Dempster Sherman.

The Voice of the Grass

Here I come creeping, creeping everywhere;
 By the dusty roadside,
 On the sunny hill-side,
 Close by the noisy brook,
 In every shady nook,
I come creeping, creeping everywhere.

Here I come creeping, smiling everywhere;
 All around the open door,
 Where sit the aged poor;
 Here where the children play,
 In the bright and merry May,
I come creeping, creeping everywhere.

THE POSY RING

Here I come creeping, creeping everywhere;
    In the noisy city street
    My pleasant face you'll meet,
    Cheering the sick at heart
    Toiling his busy part,—
Silently creeping, creeping everywhere.

Here I come creeping, creeping everywhere;
    You cannot see me coming,
    Nor hear my low sweet humming;
    For in the starry night,
    And the glad morning light,
I come quietly creeping everywhere.

Here I come creeping, creeping everywhere;
    More welcome than the flowers
    In summer's pleasant hours;
    The gentle cow is glad,
    And the merry bird not sad,
To see me creeping, creeping everywhere.

. . . .

Here I come creeping, creeping everywhere;
    My humble song of praise
    Most joyfully I raise
    To him at whose command
    I beautify the land,
Creeping, silently creeping everywhere.

                    Sarah Roberts Boyle.

The Wind in a Frolic

The wind one morning sprang up from sleep,
Saying, "Now for a frolic! Now for a leap!
Now for a madcap, galloping chase!
I'll make a commotion in every place!"
So it swept with a bustle right through a great town,
Creaking the signs, and scattering down
Shutters, and whisking, with merciless squalls,
Old women's bonnets and gingerbread stalls.
There never was heard a much lustier shout,
As the apples and oranges tumbled about;
And the urchins that stand with their thievish eyes
Forever on watch, ran off with each prize.

Then away to the field it went blustering and humming,
And the cattle all wondered whatever was coming.
It plucked by their tails the grave matronly cows,
And tossed the colts' manes all about their brows,
Till offended at such a familiar salute,
They all turned their backs and stood silently mute.
So on it went capering and playing its pranks;
Whistling with reeds on the broad river-banks;

THE POSY RING

Puffing the birds as they sat on the spray,
Or the traveller grave on the king's highway.
It was not too nice to bustle the bags
Of the beggar and flutter his dirty rags.
'Twas so bold that it feared not to play its joke
With the doctor's wig and the gentleman's cloak.
Through the forest it roared, and cried gayly,
"Now,
You sturdy old oaks, I'll make you bow!"
And it made them bow without more ado,
Or it cracked their branches through and through.

Then it rushed like a monster o'er cottage and farm,
Striking their inmates with sudden alarm;
And they ran out like bees in a midsummer swarm.
There were dames with their kerchiefs tied over their caps,
To see if their poultry were free from mishaps;
The turkeys they gobbled, the geese screamed aloud,
And the hens crept to roost in a terrified crowd;
There was rearing of ladders, and logs laying on,
Where the thatch from the roof threatened soon to be gone.
But the wind had passed on, and had met in a lane

With a schoolboy, who panted and struggled in
 vain,
For it tossed him, and twirled him, then passed,
 and he stood
With his hat in a pool and his shoe in the mud.
                              William Howitt.

Clouds

The sky is full of clouds to-day,
  And idly to and fro,
Like sheep across the pasture, they
  Across the heavens go.
I hear the wind with merry noise—
  Around the housetops sweep,
And dream it is the shepherd boys,
  They're driving home their sheep.

The clouds move faster now; and see!
  The west is red and gold.
Each sheep seems hastening to be
  The first within the fold.
I watch them hurry on until
  The blue is clear and deep,
And dream that far beyond the hill
  The shepherds fold their sheep.

Then in the sky the trembling stars
  Like little flowers shine out,

While Night puts up the shadow bars,
  And darkness falls about.
I hear the shepherd wind's good-night—
  "Good-night and happy sleep!"—
And dream that in the east, all white,
  Slumber the clouds, the sheep.

Frank Dempster Sherman.

Signs of Rain

The hollow winds begin to blow,
The clouds look black, the glass is low,
The soot falls down, the spaniels sleep,
The spiders from their cobwebs peep:
Last night the sun went pale to bed,
The moon in halos hid her head;
The boding shepherd heaves a sigh,
For, see, a rainbow spans the sky:
The walls are damp, the ditches smell,
Closed is the pink-eyed pimpernel.
Hark how the chairs and tables crack!
Old Betty's joints are on the rack;
Loud quack the ducks, the peacocks cry,
The distant hills are seeming nigh.
How restless are the snorting swine;
The busy flies disturb the kine;
Low o'er the grass the swallow wings,
The cricket too, how sharp he sings;

Puss on the hearth, with velvet paws,
Sits wiping o'er her whiskered jaws.
Through the clear stream the fishes rise,
And nimbly catch the incautious flies.
The glow-worms, numerous and bright,
Illumed the dewy dell last night.
At dusk the squalid toad was seen,
Hopping and crawling o'er the green;
The whirling wind the dust obeys,
And in the rapid eddy plays;
The frog has changed his yellow vest,
And in a russet coat is dressed.
Though June, the air is cold and still,
The mellow blackbird's voice is shrill.
My dog, so altered in his taste,
Quits mutton-bones on grass to feast;
And see yon rooks, how odd their flight,
They imitate the gliding kite,
And seem precipitate to fall,
As if they felt the piercing ball.
'Twill surely rain, I see with sorrow,
Our jaunt must be put off to-morrow.

Edward Jenner.

THE POSY RING

A Sudden Shower

Barefooted boys scud up the street,
  Or scurry under sheltering sheds;
And school-girl faces, pale and sweet,
  Gleam from the shawls about their heads.

Doors bang; and mother-voices call
  From alien homes; and rusty gates
Are slammed; and high above it all
  The thunder grim reverberates.

And then abrupt,—the rain, the rain!
  The earth lies gasping; and the eyes
Behind the streaming window-panes
  Smile at the trouble of the skies.

The highway smokes, sharp echoes ring;
  The cattle bawl and cow-bells clank;
And into town comes galloping
  The farmer's horse, with steaming flank.

The swallow dips beneath the eaves,
  And flirts his plumes and folds his wings;
And under the catawba leaves
  The caterpillar curls and clings.

The bumble-bee is pelted down
  The wet stem of the hollyhock;

And sullenly in spattered brown
   The cricket leaps the garden walk.

Within, the baby claps his hands
   And crows with rapture strange and vague;
Without, beneath the rosebush stands
   A dripping rooster on one leg.
James Whitcomb Riley.

Strange Lands

Where do you come from, Mr. Jay?
  "From the land of Play, from the land of Play."
And where can that be, Mr. Jay?
   "Far away—far away."

Where do you come from, Mrs. Dove?
  "From the land of Love, from the land of Love."
And how do you get there, Mrs. Dove?
   "Look above—look above."

Where do you come from, Baby Miss?
  "From the land of Bliss, from the land of Bliss."
And what is the way there, Baby Miss?
   "Mother's kiss—mother's kiss."
Laurence Alma Tadema.

THE POSY RING

Guessing Song

Oh ho! oh ho! Pray, who can I be?
I sweep o'er the land, I scour o'er the sea;
I cuff the tall trees till they bow down their heads,
And I rock the wee birdies asleep in their beds.
  Oh ho! oh ho! And who can I be,
    That sweep o'er the land and scour o'er the sea?

I rumple the breast of the gray-headed daw,
I tip the rook's tail up and make him cry "caw";
But though I love fun, I'm so big and so strong,
At a puff of my breath the great ships sail along.
  Oh ho! oh ho! And who can I be,
    That sweep o'er the land and sail o'er the sea?

I swing all the weather-cocks this way and that,
I play hare-and-hounds with a runaway hat;
But however I wander, I never can stray,
For go where I will, I've a free right of way!
  Oh ho! oh ho! And who can I be,
    That sweep o'er the land and scour o'er the sea?

I skim o'er the heather, I dance up the street,
I've foes that I laugh at, and friends that I greet;

I'm known in the country, I'm named in the town,
For all the world over extends my renown.
  Oh ho! oh ho! And who can I be,
  That sweep o'er the land and scour o'er the sea?

              Henry Johnstone.

The Rivulet

  Run, little rivulet, run!
  Summer is fairly begun.
Bear to the meadow the hymn of the pines,
And the echo that rings where the waterfall shines;
  Run, little rivulet, run!

  Run, little rivulet, run!
  Sing to the fields of the sun
That wavers in emerald, shimmers in gold,
Where you glide from your rocky ravine, crystal-cold;
  Run, little rivulet, run!

  Run, little rivulet, run!
  Sing of the flowers, every one,—
Of the delicate harebell and violet blue;
Of the red mountain rose-bud, all dripping with dew;
  Run, little rivulet, run!

Run, little rivulet, run!
Carry the perfume you won
From the lily, that woke when the morning was gray,
To the white waiting moonbeam adrift on the bay;
Run, little rivulet, run!

Run, little rivulet, run!
Stay not till summer is done!
Carry the city the mountain-birds' glee;
Carry the joy of the hills to the sea;
Run, little rivulet, run!
                              Lucy Larcom.

Jack Frost

The Frost looked forth on a still, clear night,
And whispered, "Now, I shall be out of sight;
So, through the valley, and over the height,
    In silence I'll take my way.
I will not go on like that blustering train,
The wind and the snow, the hail and the rain,
That make such a bustle and noise in vain;
    But I'll be as busy as they!"

So he flew to the mountain, and powdered its crest.
He lit on the trees, and their boughs he dressed

With diamonds and pearls; and over the breast
    Of the quivering lake, he spread
A coat of mail, that it need not fear
The glittering point of many a spear
Which he hung on its margin, far and near,
    Where a rock could rear its head.

He went to the window of those who slept,
And over each pane like a fairy crept:
Wherever he breathed, wherever he stepped,
    By the light of the morn were seen
Most beautiful things!—there were flowers and trees,
There were bevies of birds, and swarms of bees;
There were cities and temples and towers; and these
    All pictured in silvery sheen!

But he did one thing that was hardly fair—
He peeped in the cupboard: and finding there
That all had forgotten for him to prepare.
    "Now, just to set them a-thinking,
I'll bite this basket of fruit," said he,
"This costly pitcher I'll burst in three!
And the glass of water they've left for me,
    Shall 'tchick' to tell them I'm drinking."
                    Hannah F. Gould.

THE POSY RING

Snowflakes

Whenever a snowflake leaves the sky,
It turns and turns to say " Good-by !
Good-by, dear clouds, so cool and gray!"
Then lightly travels on its way.

And when a snowflake finds a tree,
" Good-day!" it says—" Good-day to thee!
Thou art so bare and lonely, dear,
I'll rest and call my comrades here."

But when a snowflake, brave and meek,
Lights on a rosy maiden's cheek,
It starts—" How warm and soft the day!
'Tis summer!"—and it melts away.

     Mary Mapes Dodge.

The Water! the Water!

The Water! the Water!
 The joyous brook for me,
That tuneth through the quiet night
 Its ever-living glee.
The Water! the Water!
 That sleepless, merry heart,
Which gurgles on unstintedly,
 And loveth to impart,

THE POSY RING

To all around it, some small measure
Of its own most perfect pleasure.

The Water! the Water!
  The gentle stream for me,
That gushes from the old gray stone
  Beside the alder-tree.
The Water! the Water!
  That ever-bubbling spring
I loved and look'd on while a child,
  In deepest wondering,—
And ask'd it whence it came and went,
And when its treasures would be spent.

The Water! the Water!
  The merry, wanton brook
That bent itself to pleasure me,
  Like mine old shepherd crook.
The Water! the Water!
  That sang so sweet at noon,
And sweeter still all night, to win
  Smiles from the pale proud moon,
And from the little fairy faces
That gleam in heaven's remotest places.

. . . .

William Motherwell.

III

HIAWATHA'S CHICKENS

Then the little Hiawatha
Learned of every bird its language,
Learned their names and all their secrets,
How they built their nests in Summer,
Where they hid themselves in Winter,
Talked with them whene'er he met them,
Called them " Hiawatha's Chickens."
            Henry Wadsworth Longfellow.

HIAWATHA'S CHICKENS

The Swallows

Gallant and gay in their doublets gray,
   All at a flash like the darting of flame,
Chattering Arabic, African, Indian—
   Certain of springtime, the swallows came!

Doublets of gray silk and surcoats of purple,
   And ruffs of russet round each little throat,
Wearing such garb they had crossed the waters,
   Mariners sailing with never a boat.
                         Edwin Arnold.

The Swallow's Nest

Day after day her nest she moulded,
   Building with magic, love and mud,
A gray cup made by a thousand journeys,
   And the tiny beak was trowel and hod.
                         Edwin Arnold.

THE POSY RING

The Birds in Spring

Spring, the sweet Spring, is the year's pleasant king;
Then blooms each thing, then Maids dance in a ring,
Cold doth not sting, the pretty birds do sing—
    Cuckoo, jug-jug, pu-we, to-witta-woo!

The Palm and May make country houses gay,
Lambs frisk and play, the Shepherds pipe all day,
And we hear aye birds tune this merry lay—
    Cuckoo, jug-jug, pu-we, to-witta-woo!

The Fields breathe sweet, the Daisies kiss our feet,
Young lovers meet, old wives a-sunning sit,
In every Street these Tunes our ears do greet—
    Cuckoo, jug-jug, pu-we, to-witta-woo!
    Spring, the sweet Spring!

                      Thomas Nashe.

Robin Redbreast

(A Child's Song)

Good-bye, good-bye to Summer!
  For Summer's nearly done;
The garden smiling faintly,
  Cool breezes in the sun;

THE POSY RING

Our Thrushes now are silent,
  Our Swallows flown away,—
But Robin's here, in coat of brown,
  With ruddy breast-knot gay.
Robin, Robin Redbreast,
  O Robin dear!
Robin singing sweetly
  In the falling of the year.

Bright yellow, red, and orange,
  The leaves come down in hosts;
The trees are Indian Princes,
  But soon they'll turn to Ghosts;
The scanty pears and apples
  Hang russet on the bough,
It's Autumn, Autumn, Autumn late,
  'Twill soon be Winter now.
Robin, Robin Redbreast,
  O Robin dear!
And welaway! my Robin,
  For pinching times are near.

The fireside for the Cricket,
  The wheatstack for the Mouse,
When trembling night-winds whistle
  And moan all round the house;
The frosty ways like iron,
  The branches plumed with snow,—

Alas! in Winter, dead and dark,
    Where can poor Robin go?
Robin, Robin Redbreast,
    O Robin dear!
And a crumb of bread for Robin,
    His little heart to cheer.

William Allingham.

The Lark and the Rook

"Good-night, Sir Rook!" said a little lark.
"The daylight fades; it will soon be dark;
I've bathed my wings in the sun's last ray;
I've sung my hymn to the parting day;
So now I haste to my quiet nook
In yon dewy meadow—good-night, Sir Rook!"

"Good-night, poor Lark," said his titled friend,
With a haughty toss and a distant bend;
"I also go to my rest profound,
But not to sleep on the cold, damp ground.
The fittest place for a bird like me
Is the topmost bough of yon tall pine-tree.

"I opened my eyes at peep of day
And saw you taking your upward way,
Dreaming your fond romantic dreams,
An ugly speck in the sun's bright beams;

Soaring too high to be seen or heard;
And I said to myself: 'What a foolish bird!'

" I trod the park with a princely air,
I filled my crop with the richest fare;
I cawed all day 'mid a lordly crew,
And I made more noise in the world than you!
The sun shone forth on my ebon wing;
I looked and wondered — good-night, poor thing!"

" Good-night, once more," said the lark's sweet voice.
" I see no cause to repent my choice;
You build your nest in the lofty pine,
But is your slumber more sweet than mine?
You make more noise in the world than I,
But whose is the sweeter minstrelsy?"

Unknown.

The Snowbird

In the rosy light trills the gay swallow,
The thrush, in the roses below;
The meadow-lark sings in the meadow,
But the snowbird sings in the snow.
  Ah me!
  Chickadee!
The snowbird sings in the snow!

The blue martin trills in the gable,
The wren, in the gourd below;
In the elm flutes the golden robin,
But the snowbird sings in the snow.
     Ah me!
     Chickadee!
The snowbird sings in the snow!

High wheels the gray wing of the osprey,
The wing of the sparrow drops low;
In the mist dips the wing of the robin,
And the snowbird's wing in the snow.
     Ah me!
     Chickadee!
The snowbird sings in the snow.

I love the high heart of the osprey,
The meek heart of the thrush below,
The heart of the lark in the meadow,
And the snowbird's heart in the snow.
     But dearest to me,
     Chickadee! Chickadee!
Is that true little heart in the snow.
                Hezekiah Butterworth.

THE POSY RING

Who Stole the Bird's Nest?

"To-whit! to-whit! to-whee!
Will you listen to me?
Who stole four eggs I laid,
And the nice nest I made?"

"Not I," said the cow, "Moo-oo!
Such a thing I'd never do.
I gave you a wisp of hay,
But didn't take your nest away.
Not I," said the cow, "Moo-oo!
Such a thing I'd never do."

"To-whit! to-whit! to-whee!
Will you listen to me?
Who stole four eggs I laid,
And the nice nest I made?"

"Bob-o'-link! Bob-o'-link!
Now what do you think?
Who stole a nest away
From the plum-tree, to-day?"

"Not I," said the dog, "Bow-wow!
I wouldn't be so mean, anyhow!
I gave hairs the nest to make,
But the nest I did not take.
Not I," said the dog, "Bow-wow!
I'm not so mean, anyhow."

"To-whit! to-whit! to-whee!
Will you listen to me?
Who stole four eggs I laid,
And the nice nest I made?"

"Bob-o'-link! Bob-o'-link!
Now what do you think?
Who stole a nest away
From the plum-tree, to-day?"

"Coo-coo! Coo-coo! Coo-coo!
Let me speak a word, too!
Who stole that pretty nest
From little yellow-breast?"

"Not I," said the sheep; "Oh, no!
I wouldn't treat a poor bird so.
I gave wool the nest to line,
But the nest was none of mine.
Baa! Baa!" said the sheep, "Oh, no,
I wouldn't treat a poor bird so."

"To-whit! to-whit! to-whee!
Will you listen to me?
Who stole four eggs I laid,
And the nice nest I made?"

"Bob-o'-link! Bob-o'-link!
Now what do you think?
Who stole a nest away
From the plum-tree, to-day?"

THE POSY RING

"Coo-coo! Coo-coo! Coo-coo!
Let me speak a word, too!
Who stole that pretty nest
From little yellow-breast?"

"Caw! Caw!" cried the crow;
"I should like to know
What thief took away
A bird's nest, to-day?"

"Cluck! Cluck!" said the hen;
"Don't ask me again,
Why I haven't a chick
Would do such a trick.
We all gave her a feather,
And she wove them together.
I'd scorn to intrude
On her and her brood.
Cluck! Cluck!" said the hen,
"Don't ask me again."

"Chirr-a-whirr! Chirr-a-whirr!
All the birds make a stir!
Let us find out his name,
And all cry 'For shame!'"

"I would not rob a bird,"
Said little Mary Green;
"I think I never heard
Of anything so mean."

"It is very cruel, too,"
Said little Alice Neal;
"I wonder if he knew
How sad the bird would feel?"

A little boy hung down his head,
And went and hid behind the bed,
For he stole that pretty nest
From poor little yellow-breast;
And he felt so full of shame,
He didn't like to tell his name.

Lydia Maria Child.

Answer to a Child's Question

Do you ask what the birds say? The sparrow, the dove,
The linnet, and thrush say, "I love and I love!"
In the winter they're silent, the wind is so strong;
What it says I don't know, but it sings a loud song.
But green leaves and blossoms, and sunny warm weather,
And singing and loving, all come back together;
Then the lark is so brimful of gladness and love,
The green fields below him, the blue sky above,

That he sings, and he sings, and forever sings he,
"I love my Love, and my Love loves me."
>> Samuel Taylor Coleridge.

The Burial of the Linnet

Found in the garden dead in his beauty—
  Oh that a linnet should die in the spring!
Bury him, comrades, in pitiful duty,
  Muffle the dinner-bell, solemnly ring.

Bury him kindly, up in the corner;
  Bird, beast, and goldfish are sepulchred there.
Bid the black kitten march as chief mourner,
  Waving her tail like a plume in the air.

Bury him nobly—next to the donkey;
  Fetch the old banner, and wave it about;
Bury him deeply—think of the monkey,
  Shallow his grave, and the dogs got him out.

Bury him softly—white wool around him,
  Kiss his poor feathers—the first kiss and last;
Tell his poor widow kind friends have found him:
  Plant his poor grave with whatever grows fast.

Farewell, sweet singer! dead in thy beauty,
  Silent through summer, though other birds sing.
Bury him, comrades, in pitiful duty,
  Muffle the dinner-bell, mournfully ring.
>> Juliana Horatia Ewing.

The Titmouse

. . . . Piped a tiny voice hard by,
Gay and polite, a cheerful cry,
Chic-chicadeedee! saucy note
Out of sound heart and merry throat,
As if it said, " Good-day, good sir !
Fine afternoon, old passenger!
Happy to meet you in these places,
Where January brings few faces."

This poet, though he live apart,
Moved by his hospitable heart,
Sped, when I passed his sylvan fort,
To do the honors of his court,
As fits a feathered lord of land ;
Flew near, with soft wing grazed my hand ;
Hopped on the bough, then, darting low,
Prints his small impress on the snow,
Shows feats of his gymnastic play,
Head downward, clinging to the spray,

. . . .

Here was this atom in full breath,
Hurling defiance at vast death.
This scrap of valor, just for play,
Fronts the north wind in waistcoat gray.

. . . .

Ralph Waldo Emerson.

Birds in Summer

How pleasant the life of a bird must be,
Flitting about in each leafy tree ;
In the leafy trees so broad and tall,
Like a green and beautiful palace hall,
With its airy chambers, light and boon,
That open to sun, and stars, and moon ;
That open unto the bright blue sky,
And the frolicsome winds as they wander by!

They have left their nests in the forest bough;
Those homes of delight they need not now ;
And the young and old they wander out,
And traverse the green world round about ;
And hark at the top of this leafy hall,
How, one to another, they lovingly call!
" Come up, come up!" they seem to say,
" Where the topmost twigs in the breezes play! "

" Come up, come up, for the world is fair,
Where the merry leaves dance in the summer air! "
And the birds below give back the cry,
" We come, we come to the branches high!"
How pleasant the life of the birds must be,
Living above in a leafy tree!
And away through the air what joy to go,
And to look on the green, bright earth below!

How pleasant the life of a bird must be,
Skimming about on the breezy sea,
Cresting the billows like silvery foam,
Then wheeling away to its cliff-built home!
What joy it must be to sail, upborne,
By a strong free wing, through the rosy morn,
To meet the young sun, face to face,
And pierce, like a shaft, the boundless space!

To pass through the bowers of the silver cloud;
To sing in the thunder halls aloud;
To spread out the wings for a wild, free flight
With the upper cloud-winds,—oh, what delight!
Oh, what would I give, like a bird, to go,
Right on through the arch of the sun-lit bow,
And see how the water-drops are kissed
Into green and yellow and amethyst.

How pleasant the life of a bird must be,
Wherever it listeth, there to flee;
To go, when a joyful fancy calls,
Dashing down 'mong the waterfalls;
Then wheeling about, with its mate at play,
Above and below, and among the spray,
Hither and thither, with screams as wild
As the laughing mirth of a rosy child!

What joy it must be, like a living breeze,
To flutter about 'mid the flowering trees;

Lightly to soar and to see beneath,
The wastes of the blossoming purple heath,
And the yellow furze, like fields of gold,
That gladden some fairy region old!
On mountain-tops, on the billowy sea,
On the leafy stems of the forest-tree,
How pleasant the life of a bird must be!

Mary Howitt.

An Epitaph on a Robin Redbreast

Tread lightly here; for here, 'tis said,
   When piping winds are hush'd around,
   A small note wakes from underground,
Where now his tiny bones are laid.

No more in lone or leafless groves,
   With ruffled wing and faded breast,
His friendless, homeless spirit roves;
   Gone to the world where birds are blest!

Where never cat glides o'er the green,
Or school-boy's giant form is seen;
   But love, and joy, and smiling Spring
   Inspire their little souls to sing!

Samuel Rogers.

THE POSY RING

The Bluebird

I know the song that the bluebird is singing,
Out in the apple-tree where he is swinging.
Brave little fellow! the skies may be dreary,
Nothing cares he while his heart is so cheery.

Hark! how the music leaps out from his throat!
Hark! was there ever so merry a note?
Listen awhile, and you'll hear what he's saying,
Up in the apple-tree, swinging and swaying:

"Dear little blossoms, down under the snow,
You must be weary of winter, I know;
Hark! while I sing you a message of cheer,
Summer is coming and spring-time is here!

"Little white snowdrop, I pray you arise;
Bright yellow crocus, come, open your eyes;
Sweet little violets hid from the cold,
Put on your mantles of purple and gold;
Daffodils, daffodils! say, do you hear?
Summer is coming, and spring-time is here!"

Mrs. Emily Huntington Miller.

Song

I had a dove and the sweet dove died;
    And I have thought it died of grieving:
O, what could it grieve for? Its feet were tied
    With a silken thread of my own hand's
        weaving;
Sweet little red feet! why should you die—
    Why should you leave me, sweet bird! why?
    You lived alone in the forest-tree,
Why, pretty thing! would you not live with
    me?
    I kiss'd you oft and gave you white peas;
    Why not live sweetly, as in the green trees?

                          John Keats.

What Does Little Birdie Say?

What does little birdie say,
In her nest at peep of day?
    "Let me fly," says little birdie,
"Mother, let me fly away."

Birdie, rest a little longer,
Till the little wings are stronger.
So she rests a little longer,
    Then she flies away.

What does little baby say,
In her bed at peep of day?
  Baby says, like little birdie,
"Let me rise and fly away."

Baby, sleep a little longer,
Till the little limbs are stronger.
If she sleeps a little longer,
  Baby, too, shall fly away.
                    Alfred, Lord Tennyson.

The Owl

When cats run home and light is come,
  And dew is cold upon the ground,
And the far-off stream is dumb,
  And the whirring sail goes round;
  And the whirring sail goes round;
    Alone and warming his five wits,
    The white owl in the belfry sits.

When merry milkmaids click the latch,
  And rarely smells the new-mown hay,
And the cock hath sung beneath the thatch
  Twice or thrice his roundelay,
  Twice or thrice his roundelay;
    Alone and warming his five wits,
    The white owl in the belfry sits.
                    Alfred, Lord Tennyson.

Wild Geese

The wild wind blows, the sun shines, the birds sing loud,
The blue, blue sky is flecked with fleecy dappled cloud,
Over earth's rejoicing fields the children dance and sing,
And the frogs pipe in chorus, "It is spring! It is spring!"

The grass comes, the flower laughs where lately lay the snow,
O'er the breezy hill-top hoarsely calls the crow,
By the flowing river the alder catkins swing,
And the sweet song-sparrow cries, "Spring! It is spring!"

Hark, what a clamor goes winging through the sky!
Look, children! Listen to the sound so wild and high!
Like a peal of broken bells,—kling, klang, kling,—
Far and high the wild geese cry, "Spring! It is spring!"

Bear the winter off with you, O wild geese dear!
Carry all the cold away, far away from here;

Chase the snow into the north, O strong of heart and wing,
While we share the robin's rapture, crying, "Spring! It is spring!"

       Celia Thaxter.

Chanticleer

I wake! I feel the day is near;
 I hear the red cock crowing!
He cries " 'Tis dawn!" How sweet and clear
His cheerful call comes to my ear,
 While light is slowly growing.

The white snow gathers flake on flake;
 I hear the red cock crowing!
Is anybody else awake
To see the winter morning break,
 While thick and fast 'tis snowing?

I think the world is all asleep;
 I hear the red cock crowing!
Out of the frosty pane I peep;
The drifts are piled so wide and deep,
 And wild the wind is blowing!

Nothing I see has shape or form;
 I hear the red cock crowing!

But that dear voice comes through the storm
To greet me in my nest so warm,
   As if the sky were glowing!

A happy little child, I lie
   And hear the red cock crowing.
The day is dark. I wonder why
His voice rings out so brave and high,
   With gladness overflowing.
Celia Thaxter.

The Singer

O Lark! sweet lark!
   Where learn you all your minstrelsy?
What realms are those to which you fly?
While robins feed their young from dawn till dark,
   You soar on high—
   Forever in the sky.

O child! dear child!
   Above the clouds I lift my wing
   To hear the bells of Heaven ring;
Some of their music, though my flights be wild,
   To Earth I bring;
   Then let me soar and sing!
Edmund Clarence Stedman.

The Blue Jay

O Blue Jay up in the maple-tree,
Shaking your throat with such bursts of glee,
   How did you happen to be so blue?
Did you steal a bit of the lake for your crest,
And fasten blue violets into your vest?
   Tell me, I pray you,—tell me true!

Did you dip your wings in azure dye,
When April began to paint the sky,
   That was pale with the winter's stay?
Or were you hatched from a bluebell bright,
'Neath the warm, gold breast of a sunbeam light,
   By the river one blue spring day?

O Blue Jay up in the maple-tree,
A-tossing your saucy head at me,
   With ne'er a word for my questioning,
Pray, cease for a moment your "ting-a-link,"
And hear when I tell you what I think,—
   You bonniest bit of the spring.

I think when the fairies made the flowers,
To grow in these mossy fields of ours,
   Periwinkles and violets rare,
There was left of the spring's own color, blue,
Plenty to fashion a flower whose hue
   Would be richer than all and as fair.

THE POSY RING

So, putting their wits together, they
Made one great blossom so bright and gay,
  The lily beside it seemed blurred;
And then they said, "We will toss it in air;
So many blue blossoms grow everywhere,
  Let this pretty one be a bird!"

                Susan Hartley Swett.

Robert of Lincoln

Merrily swinging on brier and weed,
  Near to the nest of his little dame,
Over the mountain-side or mead,
  Robert of Lincoln is telling his name:
      Bob-o'-link, bob-o'-link,
        Spink, spank, spink,
Snug and safe is this nest of ours,
Hidden among the summer flowers,
      Chee, chee, chee.

Robert of Lincoln is gayly drest,
  Wearing a bright, black wedding-coat;
White are his shoulders and white his crest,
  Hear him call, in his merry note,
      Bob-o'-link, bob-o'-link,
        Spink, spank, spink,

Look what a nice new coat is mine,
Sure there was never a bird so fine!
> Chee, chee, chee.

Robert of Lincoln's Quaker wife,
> Pretty and quiet, with plain brown wings,
Passing at home a patient life,
> Broods in the grass while her husband sings
>> Bob-o'-link, bob-o'-link,
>> Spink, spank, spink,
Brood, kind creature; you need not fear
Thieves and robbers while I am here,
> Chee, chee, chee.

Modest and shy as a nun is she;
> One weak chirp is her only note.
Braggart, and prince of braggarts is he,
> Pouring boasts from his little throat:
>> Bob-o'-link, bob-o'-link,
>> Spink, spank, spink,
Never was I afraid of man;
Catch me, cowardly knaves, if you can,
> Chee, chee, chee.

Six white eggs on a bed of hay,
> Flecked with purple, a pretty sight:
There as the mother sits all day,
> Robert is singing with all his might,
>> Bob-o'-link, bob-o'-link,
>> Spink, spank, spink,

THE POSY RING 77

Nice good wife, that never goes out,
Keeping house while I frolic about,
    Chee, chee, chee.

Soon as the little ones chip the shell,
  Six wide mouths are open for food;
Robert of Lincoln bestirs him well,
  Gathering seeds for the hungry brood.
    Bob-o'-link, bob-o'-link,
    Spink, spank, spink,
This new life is likely to be
Hard for a gay young fellow like me,
    Chee, chee, chee.

Robert of Lincoln at length is made
  Sober with work, and silent with care;
Off is his holiday garment laid,
  Half forgotten that merry air:
    Bob-o'-link, bob-o'-link,
    Spink, spank, spink,
Nobody knows but my mate and I
Where our nest and our nestlings lie,
    Chee, chee, chee.

Summer wanes; the children are grown;
  Fun and frolic no more he knows,
Robert of Lincoln's a humdrum crone;
  Off he flies, and we sing as he goes:
    Bob-o'-link, bob-o'-link,
    Spink, spank, spink,

When you can pipe that merry old strain,
Robert of Lincoln, come back again,
  Chee, chee, chee.

    William Cullen Bryant.

White Butterflies

Fly, white butterflies, out to sea,
Frail, pale wings for the wind to try,
Small white wings that we scarce can see,
  Fly!

Some fly light as a laugh of glee,
Some fly soft as a long, low sigh;
All to the haven where each would be,
  Fly!

   Algernon Charles Swinburne.

The Ant and the Cricket

A silly young cricket, accustomed to sing
Through the warm, sunny months of gay summer and spring,
Began to complain, when he found that at home
His cupboard was empty and winter was come.
  Not a crumb to be found
  On the snow-covered ground;

THE POSY RING

   Not a flower could he see,
   Not a leaf on a tree :
"Oh, what will become," says the cricket, " of me ? "

At last by starvation and famine made bold,
All dripping with wet and all trembling with cold,
Away he set off to a miserly ant,
To see if, to keep him alive, he would grant
   Him shelter from rain :
   A mouthful of grain
   He wished only to borrow,
   He'd repay it to-morrow :
If not, he must die of starvation and sorrow.

Says the ant to the cricket, " I'm your servant and friend,
But we ants never borrow, we ants never lend;
But tell me, dear sir, did you lay nothing by
When the weather was warm ? " Said the cricket, " Not I.
   My heart was so light
   That I sang day and night,
   For all nature looked gay."
   " You *sang*, sir, you say ?
Go then," said the ant, " and *dance* winter away."

Thus ending, he hastily lifted the wicket
And out of the door turned the poor little cricket.
Though this is a fable, the moral is good:
If you live without work, you must live without
    food.

                              Unknown.

IV

THE FLOWER FOLK

Hope is like a harebell, trembling from its birth,
Love is like a rose, the joy of all the earth;
Faith is like a lily, lifted high and white,
Love is like a lovely rose, the world's delight;
Harebells and sweet lilies show a thornless growth,
But the rose with all its thorns excels them both.

Christina G. Rossetti.

THE FLOWER FOLK

Little White Lily

Little white Lily
Sat by a stone,
Drooping and waiting
Till the sun shone.
Little white Lily
Sunshine has fed;
Little white Lily
Is lifting her head.

Little white Lily
Said, "It is good—
Little white Lily's
Clothing and food."
Little white Lily
Drest like a bride!
Shining with whiteness,
And crowned beside!

Little white Lily
Droopeth with pain,
Waiting and waiting
For the wet rain.

Little white Lily
Holdeth her cup;
Rain is fast falling
And filling it up.

Little white Lily
Said, "Good again—
When I am thirsty
To have fresh rain!
Now I am stronger;
Now I am cool;
Heat cannot burn me,
My veins are so full."

Little white Lily
Smells very sweet:
On her head sunshine,
Rain at her feet.
"Thanks to the sunshine,
Thanks to the rain!
Little white Lily
Is happy again!"

     George Macdonald.

Violets

Violets, violets, sweet March violets,
Sure as March comes, they'll come too,
First the white and then the blue—
Pretty violets!

White, with just a pinky dye,
Blue as little baby's eye,—
So like violets.

Though the rough wind shakes the house,
Knocks about the budding boughs,
There are violets.

Though the passing snow-storms come,
And the frozen birds sit dumb,
Up spring violets.

One by one among the grass,
Saying "Pluck me!" as we pass,—
Scented violets.

By and by there'll be so many,
We'll pluck dozens nor miss any:
Sweet, sweet violets!

Children, when you go to play,
Look beneath the hedge to-day:—
Mamma likes violets.

Dinah Maria Mulock.

Young Dandelion

Young Dandelion
  On a hedge-side,
Said young Dandelion,
  "Who'll be my bride?

"I'm a bold fellow
  As ever was seen,
With my shield of yellow,
  In the grass green.

"You may uproot me
  From field and from lane,
Trample me, cut me,—
  I spring up again.

"I never flinch, Sir,
  Wherever I dwell;
Give me an inch, Sir,
  I'll soon take an ell.

"Drive me from garden
  In anger and pride,
I'll thrive and harden
  By the road-side.

"Not a bit fearful,
  Showing my face,
Always so cheerful
  In every place."

THE POSY RING

Said young Dandelion,
  With a sweet air,
"I have my eye on
  Miss Daisy fair.

"Though we may tarry
  Till past the cold,
Her I will marry
  Ere I grow old.

"I will protect her
  From all kinds of harm,
Feed her with nectar,
  Shelter her warm.

"Whate'er the weather,
  Let it go by;
We'll hold together,
  Daisy and I.

"I'll ne'er give in,—no!
  Nothing I fear:
All that I win, oh!
  I'll keep for my dear."

Said young Dandelion
  On his hedge-side,
"Who'll me rely on?
  Who'll be my bride?"

     Dinah Maria Mulock.

Baby Seed Song

Little brown brother, oh! little brown brother,
   Are you awake in the dark?
Here we lie cosily, close to each other:
   Hark to the song of the lark—
"Waken!" the lark says, "waken and dress you;
   Put on your green coats and gay,
Blue sky will shine on you, sunshine caress you—
   Waken! 'tis morning—'tis May!"

Little brown brother, oh! little brown brother,
   What kind of flower will you be?
I'll be a poppy—all white, like my mother;
   Do be a poppy like me.
What! you're a sun-flower? How I shall miss you
   When you're grown golden and high!
But I shall send all the bees up to kiss you;
   Little brown brother, good-bye.

                        E. Nesbit.

A Violet Bank

I know a bank whereon the wild thyme blows,
Where oxlips and the nodding violet grows:
Quite over-canopied with lush woodbine,
With sweet musk roses and with eglantine.
                    William Shakespeare.

THE POSY RING

There's Nothing Like the Rose

The lily has an air,
  And the snowdrop a grace,
And the sweet-pea a way,
  And the heart's-ease a face,—
Yet there's nothing like the rose
  When she blows.

>> Christina G. Rossetti.

Snowdrops

Little ladies, white and green,
  With your spears about you,
Will you tell us where you've been
  Since we lived without you?

You are sweet, and fresh, and clean,
  With your pearly faces;
In the dark earth where you've been,
  There are wondrous places:

Yet you come again, serene,
  When the leaves are hidden;
Bringing joy from where you've been,
  You return unbidden—

Little ladies, white and green,
  Are you glad to cheer us?

Hunger not for where you've been,
Stay till Spring be near us!

    Laurence Alma Tadema.

Fern Song

Dance to the beat of the rain, little Fern,
And spread out your palms again,
 And say, " Tho' the sun
 Hath my vesture spun,
He had laboured, alas, in vain,
 But for the shade
 That the Cloud hath made,
And the gift of the Dew and the Rain,"
 Then laugh and upturn
 All your fronds, little Fern,
And rejoice in the beat of the rain!

    John B. Tabb.

The Violet

Down in a green and shady bed
 A modest violet grew;
Its stalk was bent, it hung its head,
 As if to hide from view.

And yet it was a lovely flower,
 Its color bright and fair;

THE POSY RING

It might have graced a rosy bower
   Instead of hiding there.

Yet there it was content to bloom,
   In modest tints arrayed;
And there diffused its sweet perfume
   Within the silent shade.

Then let me to the valley go,
   This pretty flower to see,
That I may also learn to grow
   In sweet humility.
                   Jane Taylor.

Daffy-Down-Dilly

Daffy-down-dilly
   Came up in the cold,
   Through the brown mould,
Although the March breezes
   Blew keen on her face,
Although the white snow
   Lay on many a place.

Daffy-down-dilly
   Had heard under ground,
   The sweet rushing sound
Of the streams, as they broke
   From their white winter chains,

THE POSY RING

Of the whistling spring winds,
   And the pattering rains.

"Now then," thought Daffy,
   Deep down in her heart,
   "It's time I should start."
So she pushed her soft leaves
   Through the hard frozen ground,
Quite up to the surface,
   And then she looked round.

There was snow all about her,
   Gray clouds overhead;
   The trees all looked dead:
Then how do you think
   Poor Daffy-down felt,
When the sun would not shine,
   And the ice would not melt?

"Cold weather!" thought Daffy,
   Still working away;
   "The earth's hard to-day!
There's but a half inch
   Of my leaves to be seen,
And two thirds of that
   Is more yellow than green.

"I can't do much yet;
   But I'll do what I can:
   It's well I began!

THE POSY RING

For, unless I can manage
   To lift up my head,
The people will think
   That the Spring herself's dead."

So, little by little,
   She brought her leaves out,
   All clustered about;
And then her bright flowers
   Began to unfold,
Till Daffy stood robed
   In her spring green and gold.

O Daffy-down-dilly,
   So brave and so true!
   I wish all were like you!—
So ready for duty
   In all sorts of weather,
And loyal to courage
   And duty together.

                    Anna B. Warner.

Baby Corn

A happy mother stalk of corn
   Held close a baby ear,
And whispered: "Cuddle up to me,
   I'll keep you warm, my dear.

I'll give you petticoats of green,
  With many a tuck and fold
To let out daily as you grow;
  For you will soon be old."

A funny little baby that,
  For though it had no eye,
It had a hundred mouths; 'twas well
  It did not want to cry.
The mother put in each small mouth
  A hollow thread of silk,
Through which the sun and rain and air
  Provided baby's milk.

The petticoats were gathered close
  Where all the threadlets hung.
And still as summer days went on
  To mother-stalk it clung;
And all the time it grew and grew—
  Each kernel drank the milk
By day, by night, in shade, in sun,
  From its own thread of silk.

And each grew strong and full and round
  And each was shining white;
The gores and seams were all let out,
  The green skirts fitted tight,
The ear stood straight and large and tall,
  And when it saw the sun,

THE POSY RING

Held up its emerald satin gown
   To say: "Your work is done."

"You're large enough," said Mother Stalk,
   "And now there's no more room
For you to grow." She tied the threads
   Into a soft brown plume—
It floated out upon the breeze
   To greet the dewy morn,
And then the baby said: "Now I'm
   A full-grown ear of corn!"

                       Unknown.

A Child's Fancy

O little flowers, you love me so,
   You could not do without me;
O little birds that come and go,
   You sing sweet songs about me;
O little moss, observed by few,
   That round the tree is creeping,
You like my head to rest on you,
   When I am idly sleeping.

O rushes by the river side,
   You bow when I come near you;
O fish, you leap about with pride,
   Because you think I hear you;

O river, you shine clear and bright,
  To tempt me to look in you;
O water-lilies, pure and white,
  You hope that I shall win you.

O pretty things, you love me so,
  I see I must not leave you;
You'd find it very dull, I know,
  I should not like to grieve you.
Don't wrinkle up, you silly moss;
  My flowers, you need not shiver;
My little buds, don't look so cross;
  Don't talk so loud, my river.

And I will make a promise, dears,
  That will content you, maybe;
I'll love you through the happy years,
  Till I'm a nice old lady!
True love (like yours and mine) they say
  Can never think of ceasing,
But year by year, and day by day,
  Keeps steadily increasing.

"A."

THE POSY RING

Little Dandelion

Gay little Dandelion
  Lights up the meads,
Swings on her slender foot,
  Telleth her beads,
Lists to the robin's note
  Poured from above:
Wise little Dandelion
  Asks not for love.

Cold lie the daisy banks
  Clothed but in green,
Where, in the days agone,
  Bright hues were seen.
Wild pinks are slumbering;
  Violets delay:
True little Dandelion
  Greeteth the May.

Brave little Dandelion !
  Fast falls the snow,
Bending the daffodil's
  Haughty head low.
Under that fleecy tent.
  Careless of cold,
Blithe little Dandelion
  Counteth her gold.

Meek little Dandelion
   Groweth more fair,
Till dies the amber dew
   Out from her hair.
High rides the thirsty sun,
   Fiercely and high ;
Faint little Dandelion
   Closeth her eye.

Pale little Dandelion,
   In her white shroud,
Heareth the angel breeze
   Call from the cloud!
Tiny plumes fluttering
   Make no delay!
Little winged Dandelion
   Soareth away.

                Helen B. Bostwick.

Dandelions

Upon a showery night and still,
   Without a sound of warning,
A trooper band surprised the hill,
   And held it in the morning.
We were not waked by bugle notes,
   No cheer our dreams invaded,

And yet, at dawn their yellow coats
  On the green slopes paraded.

We careless folk the deed forgot;
  'Till one day, idly walking,
We marked upon the self-same spot
  A crowd of vet'rans talking.
They shook their trembling heads and gray
  With pride and noiseless laughter;
When, well-a-day! they blew away,
  And ne'er were heard of after!

Helen Gray Cone.

The Flax Flower

Oh, the little flax flower!
  It groweth on the hill,
And, be the breeze awake or 'sleep
  It never standeth still.
It groweth, and it groweth fast;
  One day it is a seed
And then a little grassy blade
  Scarce better than a weed.
But then out comes the flax flower
  As blue as is the sky;
And " 'Tis a dainty little thing,"
  We say as we go by.

Ah! 'tis a goodly little thing,
  It groweth for the poor,
And many a peasant blesseth it
  Beside his cottage door.
He thinketh how those slender stems
  That shimmer in the sun
Are rich for him in web and woof
  And shortly shall be spun.
He thinketh how those tender flowers
  Of seed will yield him store,
And sees in thought his next year's crop
  Blue shining round his door.

Oh, the little flax flower!
  The mother then says she,
" Go, pull the thyme, the heath, the fern,
  But let the flax flower be!
It groweth for the children's sake,
  It groweth for our own;
There are flowers enough upon the hill,
  But leave the flax alone!
The farmer hath his fields of wheat,
  Much cometh to his share;
We have this little plot of flax
  That we have tilled with care."

Oh, the goodly flax flower!
  It groweth on the hill,

THE POSY RING

And, be the breeze awake or 'sleep,
   It never standeth still.
It seemeth all astir with life
   As if it loved to thrive,
As if it had a merry heart
   Within its stem alive.
Then fair befall the flax-field,
   And may the kindly showers
Give strength unto its shining stem,
   Give seed unto its flowers!

                          Mary Howitt.

Dear Little Violets

Under the green hedges after the snow,
There do the dear little violets grow,
Hiding their modest and beautiful heads
Under the hawthorn in soft mossy beds.

Sweet as the roses, and blue as the sky,
Down there do the dear little violets lie;
Hiding their heads where they scarce may be seen,
By the leaves you may know where the violet hath been.

                          John Moultrie.

Bird's Song in Spring

The silver birch is a dainty lady,
   She wears a satin gown;
The elm tree makes the old churchyard shady,
   She will not live in town.

The English oak is a sturdy fellow,
   He gets his green coat late;
The willow is smart in a suit of yellow,
   While brown the beech trees wait.

Such a gay green gown God gives the larches—
   As green as He is good!
The hazels hold up their arms for arches
   When Spring rides through the wood.

The chestnut's proud, and the lilac's pretty,
   The poplar's gentle and tall,
But the plane tree's kind to the poor dull city—
   I love him best of all!

                   E. Nesbit.

The Tree

The Tree's early leaf-buds were bursting their brown;
"Shall I take them away?" said the Frost, sweeping down.

"No, leave them alone
Till the blossoms have grown,"
Prayed the Tree, while he trembled from rootlet
    to crown.

The Tree bore his blossoms, and all the birds
    sung:
"Shall I take them away?" said the Wind, as
    he swung.
"No, leave them alone
Till the berries have grown,"
Said the Tree, while his leaflets quivering hung.

The Tree bore his fruit in the mid-summer glow:
Said the girl, "May I gather thy berries now?"
"Yes, all thou canst see:
Take them; all are for thee,"
Said the Tree, while he bent down his laden
    boughs low.

                    Björnstjerne Björnson.

The Daisy's Song

(A Fragment)

The sun, with his great eye,
Sees not so much as I;
And the moon, all silver-proud
Might as well be in a cloud.

And O the spring—the spring!
I lead the life of a king!
Couch'd in the teeming grass,
I spy each pretty lass.

I look where no one dares,
And I stare where no one stares,
And when the night is nigh
Lambs bleat my lullaby.

John Keats.

Song

For the tender beech and the sapling oak,
  That grow by the shadowy rill,
You may cut down both at a single stroke,
  You may cut down which you will.

But this you must know, that as long as they grow,
  Whatever change may be,
You can never teach either oak or beech
  To be aught but a greenwood tree.

Thomas Love Peacock.

THE POSY RING

For Good Luck

Little Kings and Queens of the May,
If you want to be,
Every one of you, very good,
In this beautiful, beautiful, beautiful wood,
Where the little birds' heads get so turned with delight
That some of them sing all night:
Whatever you pluck,
Leave some for good luck!

Picked from the stalk or pulled by the root,
From overhead or under foot,
Water-wonders of pond or brook—
Wherever you look,
And whatever you find,
Leave something behind:
Some for the Naiads,
Some for the Dryads,
And a bit for the Nixies and Pixies!

     Juliana Horatia Ewing.

V

HIAWATHA'S BROTHERS

Of all beasts he learned the language,
Learned their names and all their secrets,
How the beavers built their lodges,
Where the squirrels hid their acorns,
How the reindeer ran so swiftly,
Why the rabbit was so timid,
Talked with them whene'er he met them,
Called them "Hiawatha's Brothers."
    Henry Wadsworth Longfellow.

HIAWATHA'S BROTHERS

My Pony

My pony toss'd his sprightly head,
    And would have smiled, if smile he could,
To thank me for the slice of bread
    He thinks so delicate and good;
His eye is very bright and wild,
    He looks as if he loved me so,
Although I only am a child
    And he's a real horse, you know.

How charming it would be to rear,
    And have hind legs to balance on;
Of hay and oats within the year
    To leisurely devour a ton;
To stoop my head and quench my drouth
    With water in a lovely pail;
To wear a snaffle in my mouth,
    Fling back my ears, and slash my tail!

To gallop madly round a field,—
    Who tries to catch me is a goose,
And then with dignity to yield
    My stately back for rider's use;

To feel as only horses can,
  When matters take their proper course,
And no one notices the man,
  While loud applauses greet the horse!

He canters fast or ambles slow,
  And either is a pretty game;
His duties are but pleasures—oh,
  I wish that mine were just the same!
Lessons would be another thing
  If I might turn from book and scroll,
And learn to gallop round a ring,
  As he did when a little foal.

It must be charming to be shod,
  And beautiful beyond my praise,
When tired of rolling on the sod,
  To stand upon all-fours and graze!
Alas! my dreams are weak and wild,
  I must not ape my betters so;
Alas! I only am a child,
  And he's a real horse, you know.

"A."

THE POSY RING

On a Spaniel, called Beau,
Killing a Young Bird
(July 15, 1793)

A Spaniel, Beau, that fares like you,
   Well fed, and at his ease,
Should wiser be than to pursue
   Each trifle that he sees.

But you have kill'd a tiny bird,
   Which flew not till to-day,
Against my orders, whom you heard
   Forbidding you the prey.

Nor did you kill that you might eat,
   And ease a doggish pain,
For him, though chas'd with furious heat,
   You left where he was slain.

Nor was he of the thievish sort,
   Or one whom blood allures,
But innocent was all his sport
   Whom you have torn for yours.

My dog! What remedy remains,
   Since, teach you all I can,
I see you, after all my pains,
   So much resemble Man?

                    William Cowper.

Beau's Reply

Sir, when I flew to seize the bird
   In spite of your command,
A louder voice than yours I heard,
   And harder to withstand.

You cried—forbear!—but in my breast
   A mightier cried—proceed—
'Twas Nature, Sir, whose strong behest
   Impell'd me to the deed.

Yet much as Nature I respect,
   I ventur'd once to break,
(As you, perhaps, may recollect)
   Her precept for your sake;

And when your linnet on a day,
   Passing his prison door,
Had flutter'd all his strength away,
   And panting press'd the floor,

Well knowing him a sacred thing,
   Not destin'd to my tooth,
I only kiss'd his ruffled wing,
   And lick'd the feathers smooth.

Let my obedience *then* excuse
   My disobedience *now*,
Nor some reproof yourself refuse
   From your aggriev'd Bow-wow;

THE POSY RING

If killing birds be such a crime,
  (Which I can hardly see,)
What think you, Sir, of killing Time
  With verse address'd to me?

William Cowper.

Seal Lullaby

Oh, hush thee, my baby, the night is behind us,
  And black are the waters that sparkled so green,
The moon o'er the combers, looks downward to find us
  At rest in the hollows that rustle between.
Where billow meets billow, there soft be thy pillow;
  Ah, weary wee flipperling, curl at thy ease!
The storm shall not wake thee, nor shark overtake thee,
  Asleep in the arms of the slow-swinging seas.

Rudyard Kipling.

Milking Time

When the cows come home the milk is coming;
Honey's made while the bees are humming;
Duck and drake on the rushy lake,
And the deer live safe in the breezy brake;

And timid, funny, pert little bunny
Winks his nose, and sits all sunny.
Christina G. Rossetti.

Thank You, Pretty Cow

Thank you, pretty cow, that made
Pleasant milk to soak my bread,
Every day and every night,
Warm, and fresh, and sweet, and white.

Do not chew the hemlock rank,
Growing on the weedy bank;
But the yellow cowslip eat,
That will make it very sweet.

Where the purple violet grows,
Where the bubbling water flows,
Where the grass is fresh and fine,
Pretty cow, go there and dine.
Jane Taylor.

The Boy and the Sheep

"Lazy sheep, pray tell me why
 In the pleasant field you lie,
 Eating grass and daisies white,
 From the morning till the night:
 Everything can something do;
 But what kind of use are you?"

"Nay, my little master, nay,
Do not serve me so, I pray!
Don't you see the wool that grows
On my back to make your clothes?
Cold, ah, very cold you'd be,
If you had not wool from me.

"True, it seems a pleasant thing
Nipping daisies in the spring;
But what chilly nights I pass
On the cold and dewy grass,
Or pick my scanty dinner where
All the ground is brown and bare!

"Then the farmer comes at last,
When the merry spring is past,
Cuts my woolly fleece away,
For your coat in wintry day.
Little master, this is why
In the pleasant fields I lie."

Ann Taylor.

Lambs in the Meadow

O little lambs! the month is cold,
The sky is very gray;
You shiver in the misty grass
And bleat at all the winds that pass;

Wait! when I'm big—some day—
I'll build a roof to every fold.

But now that I am small I'll pray
At mother's knee for you;
Perhaps the angels with their wings;
Will come and warm you, little things;
I'm sure that, if God knew,
He'd let the lambs be born in May.

     Laurence Alma Tadema.

The Pet Lamb

The dew was falling fast, the stars began to blink;
I heard a voice; it said, " Drink, pretty creature, drink!"
And, looking o'er the hedge, before me I espied
A snow-white mountain-lamb, with a maiden at its side.

Nor sheep nor kine were near; the lamb was all alone.
And by a slender cord was tethered to a stone.
With one knee on the grass did the little maiden kneel,
While to that mountain-lamb she gave its evening meal.

THE POSY RING

The lamb, while from her hand he thus his supper took,
Seemed to feast, with head and ears, and his tail with pleasure shook.
"Drink, pretty creature, drink!" she said, in such a tone
That I almost received her heart into my own.

'Twas little Barbara Lewthwaite, a child of beauty rare!
I watched them with delight; they were a lovely pair.
Now with her empty can the maiden turned away,
But ere ten yards were gone her footsteps did she stay.

Right toward the lamb she looked; and from a shady place,
I, unobserved, could see the workings of her face.
If nature to her tongue could measured numbers bring,
Thus, thought I, to her lamb that little maid might sing:—

"What ails thee, young one? what? Why pull so at thy cord?
Is it not well with thee? well both for bed and board?

Thy plot of grass is soft, and green as grass can be;
Rest, little young one, rest; what is't that aileth
 thee?

"What is it thou would'st seek? What is
 wanting to thy heart?
Thy limbs, are they not strong? and beautiful
 thou art.
This grass is tender grass, these flowers they
 have no peers,
And that green corn all day is rustling in thy ears.

"If the sun be shining hot, do but stretch thy
 woollen chain,—
This beech is standing by,—its covert thou canst
 gain.
For rain and mountain storms, the like thou
 need'st not fear;
The rain and storm are things that scarcely can
 come here.

"Rest, little young one, rest; thou hast forgot
 the day
When my father found thee first, in places far
 away.
Many flocks were on the hills, but thou wert
 owned by none,
And thy mother from thy side forevermore was
 gone.

THE POSY RING

" He took thee in his arms, and in pity brought
thee home,—
A blessed day for thee!—Then whither would'st
thou roam?
A faithful nurse thou hast; the dam that did
thee yean
Upon the mountain-tops no kinder could have
been.

" Thou know'st that twice a day I have brought
thee in this can
Fresh water from the brook, as clear as ever ran;
And twice in the day, when the ground was wet
with dew,
I bring thee draughts of milk,—warm milk it is,
and new.

" Thy limbs will shortly be twice as stout as they
are now;
Then I'll yoke thee to my cart, like a pony to
the plough,
My playmate thou shalt be, and when the wind
is cold,
Our hearth shall be thy bed, our house shall be
thy fold.

"It will not, will not rest! Poor creature, can it be
That 'tis thy mother's heart which is working so
in thee?

Things that I know not of belike to thee are dear,
And dreams of things which thou canst neither see nor hear.

"Alas, the mountain-tops that look so green and fair!
I've heard of fearful winds and darkness that come there.
The little brooks, that seem all pastime and all play,
When they are angry roar like lions for their prey.

"Here thou need'st not dread the raven in the sky;
Night and day thou art safe—our cottage is hard by.
Why bleat so after me? why pull so at thy chain?
Sleep,—and at break of day I will come to thee again!"

As homeward through the lane I went with lazy feet,
This song to myself did I oftentimes repeat;
And it seemed, as I retraced the ballad line by line,
That but half of it was hers and one half of it was mine.

THE POSY RING

Again and once again did I repeat the song:
"Nay," said I, "more than half to the damsel must belong;
For she looked with such a look, and she spake with such a tone,
That I almost received her heart into my own.

William Wordsworth.

The Kitten, and Falling Leaves

See the kitten on the wall,
Sporting with the leaves that fall,
Withered leaves—one—two—and three—
From the lofty elder tree!
Through the calm and frosty air
Of this morning bright and fair,
Eddying round and round they sink
Softly, slowly: one might think
From the motions that are made,
Every little leaf conveyed
Sylph or fairy hither tending,
To this lower world descending,
Each invisible and mute,
In his wavering parachute.
But the kitten, how she starts,
Crouches, stretches, paws and darts!

First at one and then its fellow,
Just as light and just as yellow;
There are many now—now one—
Now they stop and there are none :
What intenseness of desire
In her upward eye of fire!
With a tiger-leap, half-way,
Now she meets the coming prey ;
Lets it go as fast and then
Has it in her power again.
Now she works with three or four,
Like an Indian conjuror ;
Quick as he in feats of art,
Far beyond in joy of heart.

. . . . . .

William Wordsworth.

VI

OTHER LITTLE CHILDREN

*If thou couldst know thine own sweetness,
  O little one, perfect and sweet,
Thou wouldst be a child forever;
  Completer whilst incomplete.*
                    Francis Turner Palgrave.

OTHER LITTLE CHILDREN

Where Go the Boats?

Dark brown is the river,
   Golden is the sand.
It flows along forever
   With trees on either hand.

Green leaves a-floating,
   Castles of the foam,
Boats of mine a-boating—
   Where will all come home?

On goes the river
   And out past the mill,
Away down the valley,
   Away down the hill.

Away down the river,
   A hundred miles or more,
Other little children
   Shall bring my boats ashore.
               Robert Louis Stevenson.

Cleanliness

Come, my little Robert, near—
Fie! what filthy hands are here!
Who, that e'er could understand
The rare structure of a hand,
With its branching fingers fine,
Work itself of hands divine,
Strong, yet delicately knit,
For ten thousand uses fit,
Overlaid with so clear skin
You may see the blood within,—
Who this hand would choose to cover
With a crust of dirt all over,
Till it look'd in hue and shape
Like the forefoot of an ape!
Man or boy that works or plays
In the fields or the highways,
May, without offence or hurt,
From the soil contract a dirt
Which the next clear spring or river
Washes out and out for ever—
But to cherish stains impure,
Soil deliberate to endure,
On the skin to fix a stain
Till it works into the grain,
Argues a degenerate mind,
Sordid, slothful, ill-inclined,

Wanting in that self-respect
Which does virtue best protect.
All-endearing cleanliness,
Virtue next to godliness,
Easiest, cheapest, needfull'st duty,
To the body health and beauty;
Who that's human would refuse it,
When a little water does it?
     Charles and Mary Lamb.

Wishing

Ring-ting! I wish I were a Primrose,
A bright yellow Primrose, blowing in the spring!
 The stooping bough above me,
 The wandering bee to love me,
The fern and moss to creep across,
 And the Elm-tree for our king!

Nay,—stay! I wish I were an Elm-tree,
A great lofty Elm-tree, with green leaves gay!
 The winds would set them dancing,
 The sun and moonshine glance in,
And birds would house among the boughs,
 And sweetly sing.

Oh—no! I wish I were a Robin,—
A Robin, or a little Wren, everywhere to go,

Through forest, field, or garden,
And ask no leave or pardon,
Till winter comes with icy thumbs
To ruffle up our wing!

Well,—tell! where should I fly to,
Where go sleep in the dark wood or dell?
Before the day was over,
Home must come the rover,
For mother's kiss,—sweeter this
Than any other thing.

William Allingham.

The Boy

The Boy from his bedroom window
Look'd over the little town,
And away to the bleak black upland
Under a clouded moon.

The moon came forth from her cavern.
He saw the sudden gleam
Of a tarn in the swarthy moorland;
Or perhaps the whole was a dream.

For I never could find that water
In all my walks and rides:
Far-off, in the Land of Memory,
That midnight pool abides.

Many fine things had I glimpse of,
   And said, "I shall find them one day."
Whether within or without me
   They were, I cannot say.

William Allingham.

Infant Joy

"I have no name,
I am but two days old."
What shall I call thee?
  "I happy am,
   Joy is my name."
Sweet joy befall thee!

Pretty joy!
Sweet joy but two days old!
Sweet joy I call thee.
  Thou dost smile,
  I sing the while.
Sweet joy befall thee!

William Blake

A Blessing for the Blessed

When the sun has left the hill-top
  And the daisy fringe is furled,
When the birds from wood and meadow
  In their hidden nests are curled,

Then I think of all the babies
 That are sleeping in the world.

There are babies in the high lands
 And babies in the low,
There are pale ones wrapped in furry skins
 On the margin of the snow,
And brown ones naked in the isles
 Where all the spices grow.

And some are in the palace
 On a white and downy bed,
And some are in the garret
 With a clout beneath their head,
And some are on the cold hard earth,
 Whose mothers have no bread.

O little men and women,
 Dear flowers yet unblown—
O little kings and beggars
 Of the pageant yet unshown—
Sleep soft and dream pale dreams now,
 To-morrow is your own.
                    Laurence Alma Tadema.

Piping Down the Valleys Wild

Piping down the valleys wild,
  Piping songs of pleasant glee,
On a cloud I saw a child,
  And he, laughing, said to me:

"Pipe a song about a lamb."
  So I piped with merry cheer.
"Piper, pipe that song again."
  So I piped; he wept to hear.

"Drop thy pipe, thy happy pipe,
  Sing thy songs of happy cheer."
So I sang the same again,
  While he wept with joy to hear.

"Piper, sit thee down and write,
  In a book, that all may read."—
So he vanished from my sight,
  And I plucked a hollow reed,

And I made a rural pen;
  And I stained the water clear
And I wrote my happy songs
  Every child may joy to hear.
                    William Blake.

A Sleeping Child

Lips, lips, open!
Up comes a little bird that lives inside,
Up comes a little bird, and peeps, and out he flies.

All the day he sits inside, and sometimes he sings;
Up he comes and out he goes at night to spread his wings.

Little bird, little bird, whither will you go?
Round about the world while nobody can know.

Little bird, little bird, whither do you flee?
Far away round the world while nobody can see.

Little bird, little bird, how long will you roam?
All round the world and around again home.

Round the round world, and back through the air,
When the morning comes, the little bird is there.

Back comes the little bird, and looks, and in he flies.
Up wakes the little boy, and opens both his eyes.

Sleep, sleep, little boy, little bird's away,
Little bird will come again by the peep of day;

Sleep, sleep, little boy, little bird must go
Round about the world, while nobody can know.

Sleep, sleep sound, little bird goes round,
Round and round he goes,—sleep, sleep sound!
Arthur Hugh Clough.

Birdies with Broken Wings

Birdies with broken wings,
  Hide from each other;
But babies in trouble
  Can run home to mother.
Mary Mapes Dodge.

Seven Times One

Exultation

There's no dew left on the daisies and clover,
  There's no rain left in heaven;
I've said my "seven times" over and over—
  Seven times one are seven.

I am old! so old I can write a letter;
  My birthday lessons are done:
The lambs play always, they know no better;
  They are only one times one.

O Moon! in the night I have seen you sailing,
  And shining so round and low;
You were bright! ah, bright! but your light is failing;
  You are nothing now but a bow.

You Moon! have you done something wrong in heaven,
  That God has hidden your face?
I hope, if you have, you will soon be forgiven,
  And shine again in your place.

O velvet Bee! you're a dusty fellow,
  You've powdered your legs with gold;
O brave marsh Mary-buds, rich and yellow!
  Give me your money to hold.

O Columbine! open your folded wrapper
  Where two twin turtle-doves dwell;
O Cuckoo-pint! toll me the purple clapper,
  That hangs in your clear, green bell.

And show me your nest with the young ones in it—
  I will not steal them away,
I am old! you may trust me, Linnet, Linnet,—
  I am seven times one to-day.

Jean Ingelow.

I Remember, I Remember

I remember, I remember,
  The house where I was born;
The little window where the sun
  Came peeping in at morn;
He never came a wink too soon,
  Nor brought too long a day;
But now I often wish the night
  Had borne my breath away!

I remember, I remember,
  The roses, red and white,
The violets, and the lily-cups—
  Those flowers made of light!
The lilacs where the robin built,
  And where my brother set
The laburnum, on his birthday,—
  The tree is living yet!

I remember, I remember,
  Where I was used to swing,
And thought the air must rush as fresh
  To swallows on the wing;
My spirit flew in feathers then,
  That is so heavy now.
And summer pools could hardly cool
  The fever on my brow!

I remember, I remember,
    The fir trees dark and high;
I used to think their slender tops
    Were close against the sky;
It was a childish ignorance,
    But now 'tis little joy
To know I'm farther off from heav'n
    Than when I was a boy.

                      Thomas Hood.

Good-night and Good-morning

A fair little girl sat under a tree
Sewing as long as her eyes could see;
Then smoothed her work and folded it right,
And said, "Dear work, good-night, good-night!"

Such a number of rooks came over her head
Crying, "Caw, caw!" on their way to bed;
She said, as she watched their curious flight,
"Little black things, good-night, good-night!"

The horses neighed, and the oxen lowed;
The sheep's "Bleat, bleat!" came over the road,
All seeming to say, with a quiet delight,
"Good little girl, good-night, good-night!"

She did not say to the sun, "Good-night!"
Though she saw him there like a ball of light;

THE POSY RING

For she knew he had God's own time to keep
All over the world, and never could sleep.

The tall, pink Fox-glove bowed his head—
The Violets curtsied, and went to bed;
And good little Lucy tied up her hair,
And said, on her knees, her favorite prayer.

And while on her pillow she softly lay,
She knew nothing more till again it was day,
And all things said to the beautiful sun,
"Good-morning, good-morning! our work is begun."

Lord Houghton.
(Richard Monckton Milnes.)

Little Children

Sporting through the forest wide;
Playing by the waterside;
Wandering o'er the heathy fells;
Down within the woodland dells;
All among the mountains wild,
Dwelleth many a little child!
In the baron's hall of pride;
By the poor man's dull fireside:
'Mid the mighty, 'mid the mean,
Little children may be seen,

Like the flowers that spring up fair,
Bright and countless everywhere!
In the far isles of the main;
In the desert's lone domain;
In the savage mountain-glen,
'Mong the tribes of swarthy men;
Whereso'er the sun hath shone
On a league of people'd ground,
Little children may be found!
Blessings on them! they in me
Move a kindly sympathy,
With their wishes, hopes, and fears;
With their laughter and their tears;
With their wonder so intense,
And their small experience!
Little children, not alone
On the wide earth are ye known,
'Mid its labours and its cares,
'Mid its sufferings and its snares;
Free from sorrow, free from strife,
In the world of love and life,
Where no sinful thing hath trod—
In the presence of your God,
Spotless, blameless, glorified—
Little children, ye abide!

Mary Howitt.

The Angel's Whisper

A baby was sleeping;
Its mother was weeping;
For her husband was far on the wild raging sea;
And the tempest was swelling
Round the fisherman's dwelling,
And she cried, "Dermot, darling, Oh, come back to me!"

Her beads while she numbered
The baby still slumbered,
And smiled in her face as she bended her knee.
"Oh, blest be that warning,
Thy sweet sleep adorning,
For I know that the angels are whispering to thee!

"And while they are keeping
Bright watch o'er thy sleeping,
Oh, pray to them softly, my baby, with me!
And say thou would'st rather
They'd watch o'er thy father,
For I know that the angels are whispering to thee."

The dawn of the morning
Saw Dermot returning,

And the wife wept with joy her babe's father to
  see;
  And closely caressing
  Her child with a blessing,
Said, "I knew that the angels were whispering
  to thee."

       Samuel Lover.

Little Garaine

"Where do the stars grow, little Garaine?
  The garden of moons is it far away?
The orchard of suns, my little Garaine,
  Will you take us there some day?"

"If you shut your eyes," quoth little Garaine,
  "I will show you the way to go
To the orchard of suns and the garden of moons
  And the field where the stars do grow.

"But you must speak soft," quoth little Garaine,
  "And still must your footsteps be,
For a great bear prowls in the field of stars,
  And the moons they have men to see.

"And the suns have the Children of Signs to
    guard,
  And they have no pity at all——
You must not stumble, you must not speak,
  When you come to the orchard wall.

"The gates are locked," quoth little Garaine,
  "But the way I am going to tell!
The key of your heart it will open them all
  And there's where the darlings dwell!"
                    Sir Gilbert Parker.

A Letter

(To Lady Margaret Cavendish Holles-Harley, when a Child)

My noble, lovely, little Peggy,
Let this my First Epistle beg ye,
At dawn of morn, and close of even,
To lift your heart and hands to Heaven.
In double duty say your prayer:
Our Father first, then *Notre Père*.

And, dearest child, along the day,
In every thing you do and say,
Obey and please my lord and lady,
So God shall love and angels aid ye.

If to these precepts you attend,
No second letter need I send,
And so I rest your constant friend.
                    Matthew Prior.

Love and the Child

Toys, and treats, and pleasures pass
Like a shadow in a glass,
Like the smoke that mounts on high,
Like a noonday's butterfly.

Quick they come and quick they end,
Like the money that I spend;
Some to-day, to-morrow more,
Short, like those that went before.

Mother, fold me to your knees!
How much should I care for these—
Little joys that come and go!
If you did not love me so?

And when things are sad or wrong,
Then I know that love is strong;
When I ache, or when I weep,
Then I know that love is deep.

Father, now my prayer is said,
Lay your hand upon my head!
Pleasures pass from day to day,
But I know that love will stay.

While I sleep it will be near;
I shall wake and find it here;
I shall feel it in the air
When I say my morning prayer.

THE POSY RING

Maker of this little heart!
Lord of love I know thou art!
Little heart! though thou forget,
Still the love is round thee set.

    William Brighty Rands.

Polly

Brown eyes, straight nose;
Dirt pies, rumpled clothes.

Torn books, spoilt toys:
Arch looks, unlike a boy's;

Little rages, obvious arts;
(Three her age is), cakes, tarts;

Falling down off chairs;
Breaking crown down stairs;

Catching flies on the pane;
Deep sighs—cause not plain;

Bribing you with kisses
For a few farthing blisses.

Wide-a-wake; as you hear,
" Mercy's sake, quiet, dear!"

New shoes, new frock;
Vague views of what's o'clock

When it's time to go to bed,
And scorn sublime for what is said.

Folded hands, saying prayers,
Understands not nor cares—

Thinks it odd, smiles away;
Yet may God hear her pray!

Bed gown white, kiss Dolly;
Good night!—that's Polly,

Fast asleep, as you see,
Heaven keep my girl for me!
            William Brighty Rands.

A Chill

What can lambkins do
All the keen night through?
　Nestle by their woolly mother
The careful ewe.

What can nestlings do
In the nightly dew?
　Sleep beneath their mother's wing
Till day breaks anew.

If in field or tree
There might only be
Such a warm soft sleeping-place
Found for me!
                    Christina G. Rossetti.

A Child's Laughter

All the bells of heaven may ring,
All the birds of heaven may sing,
All the wells on earth may spring,
All the winds on earth may bring
    All sweet sounds together;
Sweeter far than all things heard,
Hand of harper, tone of bird,
Sound of woods at sundawn stirred,
Welling water's winsome word,
    Wind in warm, wan weather.

One thing yet there is that none
Hearing, ere its chime be done
Knows not well the sweetest one
Heard of man beneath the sun,
    Hoped in heaven hereafter;
Soft and strong and loud and light,
Very sound of very light,
Heard from morning's rosiest height,
When the soul of all delight
    Fills a child's clear laughter.

Golden bells of welcome rolled
Never forth such note, nor told
Hours so blithe in tones so bold,
As the radiant month of gold
    Here that rings forth heaven.
If the golden-crested wren
Were a nightingale—why, then
Something seen and heard of men
Might be half as sweet as when
    Laughs a child of seven.
Algernon C. Swinburne.

The World's Music

The world's a very happy place,
  Where every child should dance and sing,
And always have a smiling face,
  And never sulk for anything.

I waken when the morning's come,
  And feel the air and light alive
With strange sweet music like the hum
  Of bees about their busy hive.

The linnets play among the leaves
  At hide-and-seek, and chirp and sing;
While, flashing to and from the eaves,
  The swallows twitter on the wing.

And twigs that shake, and boughs that sway;
   And tall old trees you could not climb;
And winds that come, but cannot stay,
   Are singing gayly all the time.

From dawn to dark the old mill-wheel
   Makes music, going round and round;
And dusty-white with flour and meal,
   The miller whistles to its sound.

The brook that flows beside the mill,
   As happy as a brook can be,
Goes singing its old song until
   It learns the singing of the sea.

For every wave upon the sands
   Sings songs you never tire to hear,
Of laden ships from sunny lands
   Where it is summer all the year.

And if you listen to the rain
   Where leaves and birds and bees are dumb,
You hear it pattering on the pane
   Like Andrew beating on his drum.

The coals beneath the kettle croon,
   And clap their hands and dance in glee;
And even the kettle hums a tune
   To tell you when it's time for tea.

The world is such a happy place
   That children, whether big or small,
Should always have a smiling face
   And never, never sulk at all.

Gabriel Setoun.

The Little Land

When at home alone I sit
And am very tired of it,
I have just to shut my eyes
To go sailing through the skies—
To go sailing far away
To the pleasant Land of Play;
To the fairy land afar
Where the Little People are;
Where the clover-tops are trees,
And the rain-pools are the seas,
And the leaves like little ships
Sail about on tiny trips;
And above the daisy tree
   Through the grasses,
High o'erhead the Bumble Bee
   Hums and passes.

THE POSY RING

In that forest to and fro
I can wander, I can go;
See the spider and the fly,
And the ants go marching by
Carrying parcels with their feet
Down the green and grassy street.
I can in the sorrel sit
Where the ladybird alit.
I can climb the jointed grass;
    And on high
See the greater swallows pass
    In the sky,
And the round sun rolling by
Heeding no such thing as I.

Through the forest I can pass
Till, as in a looking-glass,
Humming fly and daisy tree
And my tiny self I see,
Painted very clear and neat
On the rain-pool at my feet.
Should a leaflet come to land
Drifting near to where I stand,
Straight I'll board that tiny boat
Round the rain-pool sea to float.

Little thoughtful creatures sit
On the grassy coasts of it;

Little things with lovely eyes
See me sailing with surprise.
Some are clad in armour green—
(These have sure to battle been!)
Some are pied with ev'ry hue,
Black and crimson, gold and blue;
Some have wings and swift are gone;—
But they all look kindly on.

When my eyes I once again
Open and see all things plain;
High bare walls, great bare floor;
Great big knobs on drawer and door;
Great big people perched on chairs,
Stitching tucks and mending tears,
Each a hill that I could climb,
And talking nonsense all the time—
    O dear me,
      That I could be
A sailor on the rain-pool sea,
A climber in the clover-tree,
And just come back, a sleepy-head,
Late at night to go to bed.

                    Robert Louis Stevenson.

THE POSY RING

In a Garden

Baby, see the flowers!
    Baby sees
Fairer things than these,
Fairer though they be than dreams of ours.
Baby, hear the birds!
    Baby knows
Better songs than those,
Sweeter though they sound than sweetest words.

Baby, see the moon!
    Baby's eyes
Laugh to watch it rise,
Answering light with love and night with noon.

Baby, hear the sea!
    Baby's face
Takes a graver grace,
Touched with wonder what the sound may be.

Baby, see the star!
    Baby's hand
Opens, warm and bland,
Calm in claim of all things fair that are.

Baby, hear the bells!
    Baby's head
Bows as ripe for bed,
Now the flowers curl round and close their cells.

Baby, flower of light,
        Sleep and see
Brighter dreams than we,
Till good day shall smile away good night.
              Algernon Charles Swinburne.

Little Gustava

I

Little Gustava sits in the sun,
Safe in the porch, and the little drops run
From the icicles under the eaves so fast,
For the bright spring sun shines warm at last,
    And glad is little Gustava.

II

She wears a quaint little scarlet cap,
And a little green bowl she holds in her lap,
Filled with bread and milk to the brim,
And a wreath of marigolds round the rim.
    "Ha! ha!" laughs little Gustava.

III

Up comes her little gray coaxing cat
With her little pink nose, and she mews, "What's
        that?"

THE POSY RING

Gustava feeds her,—she begs for more;
And a little brown hen walks in at the door
" Good day!" cries little Gustava.

IV

She scatters crumbs for the little brown hen.
There comes a rush and a flutter, and then
Down fly her little white doves so sweet,
With their snowy wings and crimson feet:
" Welcome!" cries little Gustava.

V

So dainty and eager they pick up the crumbs.
But who is this through the doorway comes?
Little Scotch terrier, little dog Rags,
Looks in her face, and his funny tail wags:
" Ha, ha!" laughs little Gustava.

VI

" You want some breakfast too?" and down
She sets her bowl on brick floor brown;
And little dog Rags drinks up her milk,
While she strokes his shaggy locks like silk:
" Dear Rags!" says little Gustava.

VII

Waiting without stood sparrow and crow,
Cooling their feet in the melting snow:

"Won't you come in, good folk?" she cried.
But they were too bashful, and stood outside
    Though "Pray come in!" cried Gustava.

VIII

So the last she threw them, and knelt on the mat
With doves and biddy and dog and cat.
And her mother came to the open house-door
"Dear little daughter, I bring you some more.
    My merry little Gustava!"

IX

Kitty and terrier, biddy and doves,
All things harmless Gustava loves.
The shy, kind creatures 'tis joy to feed,
And oh her breakfast is sweet indeed
    To happy little Gustava!

                                Celia Thaxter.

A Bunch of Roses

The rosy mouth and rosy toe
  Of little baby brother,
Until about a month ago
  Had never met each other;
But nowadays the neighbours sweet,
  In every sort of weather,
Half way with rosy fingers meet,
  To kiss and play together.

                John B. Tabb.

The Child
At Bethlehem

Long, long before the Babe could speak,
When he would kiss his mother's cheek
  And to her bosom press,
The brightest angels standing near
Would turn away to hide a tear—
  For they are motherless.

                John B. Tabb.

After the Storm

And when,—its force expended,
The harmless storm was ended,
And as the sunrise splendid
   Came blushing o'er the sea—
I thought, as day was breaking,
My little girls were waking,
And smiling and making
   A prayer at home for me.

        William Makepeace Thackeray.

Lucy Gray

Oft I had heard of Lucy Gray;
   And, when I crossed the wild,
I chanced to see at break of day
   The solitary child.

No mate, no comrade, Lucy knew;
   She dwelt on a wide moor,—
The sweetest thing that ever grew
   Beside a human door!

You yet may spy the fawn at play,
   The hare upon the green;
But the sweet face of Lucy Gray
   Will never more be seen.

THE POSY RING

"To-night will be a stormy night—
   You to the town must go:
And take a lantern, child, to light
   Your mother through the snow."

"That, father, will I gladly do:
   'Tis scarcely afternoon—
The minster-clock has just struck two;
   And yonder is the moon."

At this the father raised his hook,
   And snapped a faggot-band;
He plied his work;—and Lucy took
   The lantern in her hand.

Not blither is the mountain roe:
   With many a wanton stroke
Her feet disperse the powdery snow,
   That rises up like smoke.

The storm came on before its time
   She wandered up and down;
And many a hill did Lucy climb,
   But never reached the town.

The wretched parents all that night
   Went shouting far and wide;
But there was neither sound nor sight
   To serve them for a guide.

At daybreak on a hill they stood
  That overlooked the moor;
And thence they saw the bridge of wood,
  A furlong from their door.

They wept—and, turning homeward, cried,
  " In heaven we all shall meet! "
When in the snow the mother spied
  The print of Lucy's feet.

Then downwards from the steep hill's edge
  They tracked the footmarks small;
And through the broken hawthorn hedge,
  And by the low stone wall:

And then an open field they crossed;
  The marks were still the same;
They tracked them on, nor ever lost;
  And to the bridge they came.

They follow from the snowy bank
  Those footmarks, one by one,
Into the middle of the plank;
  And further there were none!

—Yet some maintain that to this day
  She is a living child;
That you may see sweet Lucy Gray
  Upon the lonesome wild.

O'er rough and smooth she trips along,
   And never looks behind;
And sings a solitary song
   That whistles in the wind.

William Wordsworth

Deaf and Dumb

He lies on the grass, looking up to the sky;
Blue butterflies pass like a breath or a sigh,
The shy little hare runs confidingly near,
And wise rabbits stare with inquiry, not fear:
Gay squirrels have found him and made him their choice;
All creatures flock round him, and seem to rejoice.

Wild ladybirds leap on his cheek fresh and fair,
Young partridges creep, nestling under his hair,
Brown honey-bees drop something sweet on his lips,
Rash grasshoppers hop on his round finger-tips,
Birds hover above him with musical call;
All things seem to love him, and he loves them all.

Is nothing afraid of the boy lying there?
Would all nature aid if he wanted its care?

Things timid and wild with soft eagerness come.
Ah, poor little child!—he is deaf—he is dumb.
But what can have brought them? but how can they know?
What instinct has taught them to cherish him so?

Since first he could walk they have served him like this.
His lips could not talk, but they found they could kiss.
They made him a court, and they crowned him a king;
Ah, who could have thought of so lovely a thing?
They found him so pretty, they gave him their hearts,
And some divine pity has taught them their parts!

"A."

The Blind Boy

O, say, what is that thing called Light,
   Which I must ne'er enjoy?
What are the blessings of the sight?
   O tell your poor blind boy!

You talk of wondrous things you see;
   You say the sun shines bright;

THE POSY RING

I feel him warm, but how can he
  Make either day or night?

My day and night myself I make,
  Whene'er I sleep or play,
And could I always keep awake,
  With me 'twere always day.

With heavy sighs I often hear
  You mourn my hapless woe;
But sure with patience I can bear
  A loss I ne'er can know.

Then let not what I cannot have
  My peace of mind destroy;
Whilst thus I sing, I am a king,
  Although a poor blind boy!

                    Colley Cibber.

VII

PLAY-TIME

The world's a very happy place,
  Where every child should dance and sing,
And always have a smiling face,
  And never sulk for anything.
                    Gabriel Setoun.

PLAY-TIME

A Boy's Song

Where the pools are bright and deep,
Where the gray trout lies asleep,
Up the river and o'er the lea,
That's the way for Billy and me.

Where the blackbird sings the latest,
Where the hawthorn blooms the sweetest,
Where the nestlings chirp and flee,
That's the way for Billy and me.

Where the mowers mow the cleanest,
Where the hay lies thick and greenest,
There to trace the homeward bee,
That's the way for Billy and me.

Where the hazel bank is steepest,
Where the shadow falls the deepest,
Where the clustering nuts fall free,
That's the way for Billy and me.

Why the boys should drive away
Little sweet maidens from the play,
Or love to banter and fight so well,
That's the thing I never could tell.

But this I know, I love to play,
Through the meadow, among the hay;
Up the water and o'er the lea,
That's the way for Billy and me.

  James Hogg (The Ettrick Shepherd).

The Lost Doll

I once had a sweet little doll, dears,
 The prettiest doll in the world;
Her cheeks were so red and white, dears,
 And her hair was so charmingly curled.
But I lost my poor little doll, dears,
 As I played on the heath one day;
And I cried for her more than a week, dears,
 But I never could find where she lay.

I found my poor little doll, dears,
 As I played on the heath one day;
Folks say she is terribly changed, dears,
 For her paint is all washed away,
And her arms trodden off by the cows, dears,
 And her hair not the least bit curled;
Yet for old sake's sake, she is still, dears,
 The prettiest doll in the world.

      Charles Kingsley.

Dolladine

This is her picture—Dolladine—
The beautifullest doll that ever was seen!
Oh, what nosegays! Oh, what sashes!
Oh, what beautiful eyes and lashes!

Oh, what a precious perfect pet!
On each instep a pink rosette;
Little blue shoes for her little blue tots;
Elegant ribbons in bows and knots.

Her hair is powdered; her arms are straight,
Only feel, she is quite a weight!
Her legs are limp, though;—stand up, miss!—
What a beautiful buttoned-up mouth to kiss!
     William Brighty Rands.

Dressing the Doll

This is the way we dress the Doll:—
You may make her a shepherdess, the Doll,
If you give her a crook with a pastoral hook,
But this is the way we dress the Doll.

Chorus.

Bless the Doll, you may press the Doll,
But do not crumple and mess the Doll!
This is the way we dress the Doll.

First, you observe her little chemise,
As white as milk, with ruches of silk;
And the little drawers that cover her knees,
As she sits or stands, with golden bands,
And lace in beautiful filagrees.

CHORUS.

Bless the Doll, you may press the Doll,
But do not crumple or mess the Doll!
This is the way we dress the Doll.

Now these are the bodies: she has two,
One of pink, with ruches of blue,
And sweet white lace; be careful, do!
And one of green, with buttons of sheen,
Buttons and bands of gold, I mean,
With lace on the border in lovely order,
The most expensive we can afford her!

CHORUS.

Bless the Doll, you may press the Doll,
But do not crumple or mess the Doll!
This is the way we dress the Doll.

Then, with black at the border, jacket
And this—and this—she will not lack it;
Skirts? Why, there are skirts, of course,
And shoes and stockings we shall enforce,

With a proper bodice, in the proper place
(Stays that lace have had their days
And made their martyrs); likewise garters,
All entire. But our desire
Is to show you her night attire,
At least a part of it. Pray admire
This sweet white thing that she goes to bed in!
It's not the one that's made for her wedding;
That is special, a new design,
Made with a charm and a countersign,
Three times three and nine times nine:
These are only her usual clothes:
Look, *there's* a wardrobe! gracious knows
It's pretty enough, as far as it goes!

So you see the way we dress the Doll:
You might make her a shepherdess, the Doll,
If you gave her a crook with a pastoral hook,
With sheep, and a shed, and a shallow brook,
And all that, out of the poetry-book.

CHORUS.

Bless the Doll, you may press the Doll,
But do not crumple and mess the Doll!
This is the way we dress the Doll;
If you had not seen, could you guess the Doll?

William Brighty Rands.

The Pedlar's Caravan

I wish I lived in a caravan,
With a horse to drive, like a pedlar-man!
Where he comes from nobody knows,
Or where he goes to, but on he goes!

His caravan has windows two,
And a chimney of tin, that the smoke comes
 through;
He has a wife, with a baby brown,
And they go riding from town to town.

Chairs to mend, and delf to sell!
He clashes the basins like a bell;
Tea-trays, baskets ranged in order,
Plates with the alphabet round the border!

The roads are brown, and the sea is green,
But his house is just like a bathing-machine;
The world is round, and he can ride,
Rumble and splash, to the other side!

With the pedlar-man I should like to roam,
And write a book when I came home;
All the people would read my book,
Just like the Travels of Captain Cook!

William Brighty Rands.

A Sea-Song from the Shore

    Hail! Ho!
    Sail! Ho!
Ahoy! Ahoy! Ahoy!
    Who calls to me,
    So far at sea?
Only a little boy!

    Sail! Ho!
    Hail! Ho!
The sailor he sails the sea:
    I wish he would capture a little sea-horse
And send him home to me.

    I wish, as he sails
    Through the tropical gales,
He would catch me a sea-bird, too,
    With its silver wings
    And the song it sings,
And its breast of down and dew!

    I wish he would catch me a
    Little mermaid,
Some island where he lands,
    With her dripping curls,
    And her crown of pearls,
And the looking-glass in her hands!

Hail! Ho!
Sail! Ho!
Sail far o'er the fabulous main!
And if I were a sailor,
I'd sail with you,
Though I never sailed back again.

James Whitcomb Riley.

The Land of Story-Books

At evening when the lamp is lit,
Around the fire my parents sit;
They sit at home and talk and sing,
And do not play at anything.

Now, with my little gun, I crawl
All in the dark along the wall,
And follow round the forest track
Away behind the sofa back.

There, in the night, where none can spy,
All in my hunter's camp I lie,
And play at books that I have read
Till it is time to go to bed.

These are the hills, these are the woods,
These are my starry solitudes;
And there the river by whose brink
The roaring lions come to drink.

I see the others far away
As if in firelit camp they lay,
And I, like to an Indian scout,
Around their party prowled about.

So, when my nurse comes in for me,
Home I return across the sea,
And go to bed with backward looks
At my dear land of Story-books.

     Robert Louis Stevenson.

The City Child

Dainty little maiden, whither would you wander?
Whither from this pretty home, the home where
  mother dwells?
" Far and far away," said the dainty little maiden,
" All among the gardens, auriculas, anemones,
Roses and lilies and Canterbury bells."

Dainty little maiden, whither would you wander?
Whither from this pretty house, this city-house
  of ours?
" Far and far away," said the dainty little maiden,
" All among the meadows, the clover and the
  clematis,
Daisies and kingcups and honeysuckle-flowers."

     Alfred, Lord Tennyson.

Going into Breeches

Joy to Philip! he this day
Has his long coats cast away,
And (the childish season gone)
Put the manly breeches on.
Officer on gay parade,
Red-coat in his first cockade,
Bridegroom in his wedding-trim,
Birthday beau surpassing him,
Never did with conscious gait
Strut about in half the state
Or the pride (yet free from sin)
Of my little MANIKIN:
Never was there pride or bliss
Half so rational as his.
Sashes, frocks, to those that need 'em,
Philip's limbs have got their freedom—
He can run, or he can ride,
And do twenty things beside,
Which his petticoats forbade;
Is he not a happy lad?
Now he's under other banners
He must leave his former manners;
Bid adieu to female games
And forget their very names;
Puss-in-corners, hide-and-seek,
Sports for girls and punies weak!

Baste-the-bear he now may play at;
Leap-frog, foot-ball sport away at;
Show his skill and strength at cricket,
Mark his distance, pitch his wicket;
Run about in winter's snow
Till his cheeks and fingers glow;
Climb a tree or scale a wall
Without any fear to fall.
If he get a hurt or bruise,
To complain he must refuse,
Though the anguish and the smart
Go unto his little heart;
He must have his courage ready,
Keep his voice and visage steady;
Brace his eyeballs stiff as drum,
That a tear may never come;
And his grief must only speak
From the colour in his cheek.
This and more he must endure,
Hero he in miniature.
This and more must now be done,
Now the breeches are put on.

     Charles and Mary Lamb.

THE POSY RING

Hunting Song

Up, up! ye dames and lasses gay!
To the meadows trip away.
'Tis you must tend the flocks this morn,
And scare the small birds from the corn,
    Not a soul at home may stay:
        For the shepherds must go
        With lance and bow
    To hunt the wolf in the woods to-day.

Leave the hearth and leave the house
To the cricket and the mouse:
Find grannam out a sunny seat,
With babe and lambkin at her feet.
    Not a soul at home may stay:
        For the shepherds must go
        With lance and bow
    To hunt the wolf in the woods to-day.

                Samuel Taylor Coleridge.

Hie Away

Hie away, hie away!
Over bank and over brae,
Where the copsewood is the greenest,
Where the fountains glisten sheenest,
Where the lady fern grows strongest,
Where the morning dew lies longest,

Where the blackcock sweetest sips it,
Where the fairy latest trips it:
Hie to haunts right seldom seen,
Lovely, lonesome, cool, and green,
Over bank and over brae,
Hie away, hie away!

       Sir Walter Scott.

VIII

STORY TIME

And I made a rural pen;
  And I stained the water clear
And I wrote my happy songs
  Every child may joy to hear.
                    William Blake.

STORY TIME

The Fairy Folk

Come cuddle close in daddy's coat
   Beside the fire so bright,
And hear about the fairy folk
   That wander in the night.
For when the stars are shining clear
   And all the world is still,
They float across the silver moon
   From hill to cloudy hill.

Their caps of red, their cloaks of green,
   Are hung with silver bells,
And when they're shaken with the wind
   Their merry ringing swells.
And riding on the crimson moth,
   With black spots on his wings,
They guide them down the purple sky
   With golden bridle rings.

They love to visit girls and boys
   To see how sweet they sleep,
To stand beside their cosy cots
   And at their faces peep.
For in the whole of fairy land
   They have no finer sight
Than little children sleeping sound
   With faces rosy bright.

On tip-toe crowding round their heads,
   When bright the moonlight beams,
They whisper little tender words
   That fill their minds with dreams;
And when they see a sunny smile,
   With lightest finger tips
They lay a hundred kisses sweet
   Upon the ruddy lips.

And then the little spotted moths
   Spread out their crimson wings,
And bear away the fairy crowd
   With shaking bridle rings.
Come bairnies, hide in daddy's coat,
   Beside the fire so bright—
Perhaps the little fairy folk
   Will visit you to-night.

                       Robert Bird.

A Fairy in Armor

He put his acorn helmet on;
It was plumed of the silk of the thistle down;
The corslet plate that guarded his breast
Was once the wild bee's golden vest;
His cloak, of a thousand mingled dyes,
Was formed of the wings of butterflies;
His shield was the shell of a lady-bug green,
Studs of gold on a ground of green;
And the quivering lance which he brandished bright,
Was the sting of a wasp he had slain in fight.
Swift he bestrode his fire-fly steed;
  He bared his blade of the bent-grass blue;
He drove his spurs of the cockle-seed,
  And away like a glance of thought he flew,
To skim the heavens, and follow far
The fiery trail of the rocket-star.

Joseph Rodman Drake.

The Last Voyage of the Fairies

Down the bright stream the Fairies float,—
A water-lily is their boat.

Long rushes they for paddles take,
Their mainsail of a bat's wing make;

The tackle is of cobwebs neat,—
With glow-worm lantern all's complete.

So down the broad'ning stream they float,
With Puck as pilot of the boat.

The Queen on speckled moth-wings lies,
And lifts at times her languid eyes

To mark the green and mossy spots
Where bloom the blue forget-me-nots:

Oberon, on his rose-bud throne,
Claims the fair valley as his own:

And elves and fairies, with a shout
Which may be heard a yard about,

Hail him as Elfland's mighty King;
And hazel-nuts in homage bring,

And bend the unreluctant knee,
And wave their wands in loyalty.

THE POSY RING

Down the broad stream the Fairies float,
An unseen power impels their boat;

The banks fly past—each wooded scene—
The elder copse—the poplars green—

And soon they feel the briny breeze
With salt and savour of the seas—

Still down the stream the Fairies float,
An unseen power impels their boat;

Until they mark the rushing tide
Within the estuary wide.

And now they're tossing on the sea,
Where waves roll high, and winds blow free,—

Ah, mortal vision nevermore
Shall see the Fairies on the shore,

Or watch upon a summer night
Their mazy dances of delight!

Far, far away upon the sea,
The waves roll high, the breeze blows free!

The Queen on speckled moth-wings lies,
Slow gazing with a strange surprise

Where swim the sea-nymphs on the tide
Or on the backs of dolphins ride:

The King, upon his rose-bud throne,
Pales as he hears the waters moan;

The elves have ceased their sportive play,
Hushed by the slowly sinking day:

And still afar, afar they float,
The Fairies in their fragile boat,—

Further and further from the shore,
And lost to mortals evermore!

W. H. Davenport Adams.

A New Fern

A Fairy has found a new fern!
　A lovely surprise of the May!
She stamps her wee foot, looks uncommonly stern,
　And keeps other fairies at bay.

She watches it flourish and grow—
　What exquisite pleasure is hers!
She kisses it, strokes it and fondles it so—
　I almost believe that she purrs!

Of all the most beautiful things,
　None brighter than this I discern,
To be a young fairy, with glittering wings,
　And then—to discover a fern!

"A."

The Child and the Fairies

The woods are full of fairies!
  The trees are all alive:
The river overflows with them,
  See how they dip and dive!
What funny little fellows!
  What dainty little dears!
They dance and leap, and prance and peep,
  And utter fairy cheers!

. . . . . .

I'd like to tame a fairy,
  To keep it on a shelf,
To see it wash its little face,
  And dress its little self.
I'd teach it pretty manners,
  It always should say "Please;"
And then you know I'd make it sew,
  And curtsey with its knees!

              "A."

The Little Elf

I met a little Elf-man, once,
   Down where the lilies blow.
I asked him why he was so small
   And why he didn't grow.

He slightly frowned, and with his eye
   He looked me through and through.
"I'm quite as big for me," said he,
   "As you are big for you."

John Kendrick Bangs.

"One, Two, Three"

It was an old, old, old, old lady
   And a boy that was half-past three,
And the way that they played together
   Was beautiful to see.

She couldn't go romping and jumping,
   And the boy, no more could he;
For he was a thin little fellow,
   With a thin little twisted knee.

They sat in the yellow sunlight,
   Out under the maple tree,
And the game that they played I'll tell you,
   Just as it was told to me.

THE POSY RING

It was Hide-and-Go-Seek they were playing.
  Though you'd never have known it to be—
With an old, old, old, old lady
  And a boy with a twisted knee.

The boy would bend his face down
  On his little sound right knee.
And he guessed where she was hiding
  In guesses One, Two, Three.

"You are in the china closet!"
  He would cry and laugh with glee—
It wasn't the china closet,
  But he still had Two and Three.

"You are up in papa's big bedroom,
  In the chest with the queer old key,"
And she said: "You are warm and warmer;
  But you are not quite right," said she.

"It can't be the little cupboard
  Where mamma's things used to be—
So it must be in the clothes press, Gran'ma,"
  And he found her with his Three.

Then she covered her face with her fingers,
  That were wrinkled and white and wee,
And she guessed where the boy was hiding,
  With a One and a Two and a Three.

And they never had stirred from their places
  Right under the maple tree—
This old, old, old, old lady
  And the boy with the lame little knee—
This dear, dear, dear old lady
  And the boy who was half-past three.

      Henry C. Bunner.

What May Happen to a Thimble

Come about the meadow,
  Hunt here and there,
Where's mother's thimble?
  Can you tell where?
Jane saw her wearing it,
  Fan saw it fall,
Ned isn't sure
  That she dropp'd it at all.

Has a mouse carried it
  Down to her hole—
Home full of twilight,
  Shady, small soul?
Can she be darning there,
  Ere the light fails,
Small ragged stockings—
  Tiny torn tails?

THE POSY RING

Did a finch fly with it
  Into the hedge,
Or a reed-warbler
  Down in the sedge?
Are they carousing there,
  All the night through?
Such a great goblet,
  Brimful of dew!

Have beetles crept with it
  Where oak roots hide?
There have they settled it
  Down on its side?
Neat little kennel,
  So cosy and dark,
Has one crept into it,
  Trying to bark?

Have the ants cover'd it
  With straw and sand?
Roomy bell-tent for them,
  So tall and grand;
Where the red soldier-ants
  Lie, loll, and lean—
While the blacks steadily
  Build for their queen.

Has a huge dragon-fly
  Borne it (how cool!)

To his snug dressing-room,
  By the clear pool?
There will he try it on,
  For a new hat—
Nobody watching
  But one water-rat?

Did the flowers fight for it,
  While, undecried,
One selfish daisy
  Slipp'd it aside;
Now has she plunged it in
  Close to her feet—
Nice private water-tank
  For summer heat?

Did spiders snatch at it
  Wanting to look
At the bright pebbles
  Which lie in the brook?
Now are they using it
  (Nobody knows!)
Safe little diving-bell,
  Shutting so close?

Hunt for it, hope for it,
  All through the moss;
Dip for it, grope for it—
  'Tis such a loss!

Jane finds a drop of dew,
  Fan finds a stone;
I find the thimble,
  Which is mother's own!

Run with it, fly with it—
  Don't let it fall;
All did their best for it—
  Mother thanks all.
Just as we give it her,—
  Think what a shame!—
Ned says he's sure
  That it isn't the same!

"B."

Discontent

Down in a field, one day in June,
  The flowers all bloomed together,
Save one, who tried to hide herself,
  And drooped that pleasant weather.

A robin, who had flown too high,
  And felt a little lazy,
Was resting near a buttercup
  Who wished she were a daisy.

For daisies grew so trig and tall!
  She always had a passion
For wearing frills around her neck,
  In just the daisies' fashion.

And buttercups must always be
  The same old tiresome color;
While daisies dress in gold and white,
  Although their gold is duller.

"Dear robin," said the sad young flower,
  "Perhaps you'd not mind trying
To find a nice white frill for me,
  Some day when you are flying?"

"You silly thing!" the robin said,
  "I think you must be crazy:
I'd rather be my honest self,
  Than any made-up daisy.

"You're nicer in your own bright gown;
  The little children love you:
Be the best buttercup you can,
  And think no flower above you.

"Though swallows leave me out of sight,
  We'd better keep our places:
Perhaps the world would all go wrong
  With one too many daisies.

"Look bravely up into the sky,
  And be content with knowing
That God wished for a buttercup
  Just here, where you are growing."

Sarah Orne Jewett.

The Nightingale and the Glowworm

A nightingale that all day long
Had cheered the village with his song,
Nor yet at eve his note suspended,
Nor yet when eventide was ended,
Began to feel, as well he might,
The keen demands of appetite;
When looking eagerly around,
He spied far off, upon the ground,
A something shining in the dark,
And knew the glowworm by his spark;
So, stooping down from hawthorn top,
He thought to put him in his crop.

The worm, aware of his intent,
Harangued him thus, right eloquent:
"Did you admire my lamp," quoth he,
"As much as I your minstrelsy,
You would abhor to do me wrong,
As much as I to spoil your song:

For 'twas the self-same Power Divine
Taught you to sing, and me to shine;
That you with music, I with light,
Might beautify and cheer the night."
The songster heard this short oration,
And warbling out his approbation,
Released him, as my story tells,
And found a supper somewhere else.

William Cowper.

Thanksgiving Day

Over the river and through the wood,
  To grandfather's house we go;
    The horse knows the way
    To carry the sleigh
  Through the white and drifted snow.
Over the river and through the wood—
  Oh, how the wind does blow!
    It stings the toes
    And bites the nose,
  As over the ground we go.

Over the river and through the wood,
  To have a first-rate play.
    Hear the bells ring,
    "Ting-a-ling-ding!"
  Hurrah for Thanksgiving Day!

THE POSY RING

Over the river and through the wood
   Trot fast, my dapple-gray!
     Spring over the ground,
     Like a hunting-hound!
   For this is Thanksgiving Day.

Over the river and through the wood,
   And straight through the barn-yard gate.
     We seem to go
     Extremely slow,—
   It is so hard to wait!

Over the river and through the wood—
   Now grandmother's cap I spy!
     Hurrah for the fun!
     Is the pudding done?
   Hurrah for the pumpkin-pie?

                Lydia Maria Child.

A Thanksgiving Fable

It was a hungry pussy cat, upon Thanksgiving morn,
And she watched a thankful little mouse, that ate an ear of corn.
"If I ate that thankful little mouse, how thankful he should be,
When he has made a meal himself, to make a meal for me!

"Then with his thanks for having fed, and his
    thanks for feeding me,
With all *his* thankfulness inside, how thankful I
    shall be!"
Thus mused the hungry pussy cat, upon Thanks-
    giving Day;
But the little mouse had overheard and declined
    (with thanks) to stay.

                          Oliver Herford.

The Magpie's Nest
A Fable

When the Arts in their infancy were,
   In a fable of old 'tis express'd
A wise magpie constructed that rare
   Little house for young birds, call'd a nest.

This was talk'd of the whole country round;
   You might hear it on every bough sung,
"Now no longer upon the rough ground
   Will fond mothers brood over their young:

"For the magpie with exquisite skill
   Has invented a moss-cover'd cell
Within which a whole family will
   In the utmost security dwell."

THE POSY RING

To her mate did each female bird say,
  "Let us fly to the magpie, my dear;
If she will but teach us the way,
  A nest we will build us up here.

"It's a thing that's close arch'd overhead,
  With a hole made to creep out and in;
We, my bird, might make just a bed
  If we only knew how to begin."

. . . . . .

To the magpie soon every bird went
  And in modest terms made their request,
That she would be pleased to consent
  To teach them to build up a nest.

She replied, "I will show you the way,
  So observe everything that I do:
First two sticks 'cross each other I lay—"
  "To be sure," said the crow, "why I knew

"It must be begun with two sticks,
  And I thought that they crossed should be."
Said the pie, "Then some straw and moss mix
  In the way you now see done by me."

"O yes, certainly," said the jackdaw,
  "That must follow, of course, I have thought;
Though I never before building saw,
  I guess'd that, without being taught."

"More moss, straw, and feathers, I place
   In this manner," continued the pie.
"Yes, no doubt, madam, that is the case;
   Though no builder myself, so thought I."

. . . . . .

Whatever she taught them beside,
   In his turn every bird of them said,
Though the nest-making art he ne'er tried
   He had just such a thought in his head.

Still the pie went on showing her art,
   Till a nest she had built up half-way;
She no more of her skill would impart,
   But in her anger went fluttering away.

And this speech in their hearing she made,
   As she perch'd o'er their heads on a tree:
"If ye all were well skill'd in my trade,
   Pray, why came ye to learn it of me?"

When a scholar is willing to learn,
   He with silent submission should hear;
Too late they their folly discern,
   The effect to this day does appear.

For whenever a pie's nest you see,
   Her charming warm canopy view,

All birds' nests but hers seem to be
  A magpie's nest just cut in two.
                Charles and Mary Lamb.

The Owl and the Pussy-Cat

The Owl and the Pussy-Cat went to sea
  In a beautiful pea-green boat;
They took some honey, and plenty of money
  Wrapped up in a five-pound note.
The Owl looked up to the moon above,
  And sang to a small guitar,
"O lovely Pussy! O Pussy, my love,
  What a beautiful Pussy you are,—
        You are,
What a beautiful Pussy you are!"

Pussy said to the Owl, "You elegant fowl!
  How wonderful sweet you sing!
O let us be married,—too long we have tarried,—
  But what shall we do for a ring?"
They sailed away for a year and a day
  To the land where the Bong tree grows
And there in a wood, a piggy-wig stood

With a ring at the end of his nose,—
>   His nose,
With a ring at the end of his nose.

"Dear Pig, are you willing to sell for one shilling
>   Your ring?" Said the piggy, "I will."
So they took it away, and were married next day
>   By the turkey who lives on the hill.
They dined upon mince and slices of quince,
>   Which they ate with a runcible spoon,
And hand in hand on the edge of the sand
>   They danced by the light of the moon,—
>   The moon,
They danced by the light of the moon.

Edward Lear.

A Lobster Quadrille

"Will you walk a little faster?" said a whiting
to a snail,
"There's a porpoise close behind us, and he's
treading on my tail.
See how eagerly the lobsters and the turtles all
advance!
They are waiting on the shingle—will you come
and join the dance?
Will you, won't you, will you, won't you, will
you join the dance?

Will you, won't you, will you, won't you, won't
you join the dance?

"You can really have no notion how delight-
ful it will be
When they take us up and throw us, with the
lobsters, out to sea!"
But the snail replied, "Too far, too far!" and
gave a look askance—
Said he thanked the whiting kindly, but he
would not join the dance.
Would not, could not, would not, could not,
would not join the dance,
Would not, could not, would not, could not,
could not join the dance.

"What matters it how far we go?" his scaly
friend replied,
"There is another shore, you know, upon the
other side.
The further off from England the nearer is to
France—
Then turn not pale, beloved snail, but come and
join the dance.
Will you, won't you, will you, won't you, will
you join the dance?
Will you, won't you, will you, won't you, won't
you join the dance?"

Lewis Carroll.

The Fairies' Shopping

Where do you think the Fairies go
To buy their blankets ere the snow?

When Autumn comes, with frosty days
The sorry shivering little Fays

Begin to think it's time to creep
Down to their caves for Winter sleep.

But first they come from far and near
To buy, where shops are not too dear.

(The wind and frost bring prices down,
So Fall's their time to come to town!)

Where on the hill-side rough and steep
Browse all day long the cows and sheep,

The mullein's yellow candles burn
Over the heads of dry sweet fern:

All summer long the mullein weaves
His soft and thick and woolly leaves.

Warmer blankets were never seen
Than these broad leaves of fuzzy green—

(The cost of each is but a shekel
Made from the gold of honeysuckle!)

THE POSY RING

To buy their sheets and fine white lace
(With which to trim a pillow-case),

They only have to go next door,
Where stands a sleek brown spider's store,

And there they find the misty threads
Ready to cut into sheets and spreads;

Then for a pillow, pluck with care
Some soft-winged seeds as light as air;

Just what they want the thistle brings,
But thistles are such surly things—

And so, though it is somewhat high,
The clematis the Fairies buy.

The only bedsteads that they need
Are silky pods of ripe milk-weed,

With hangings of the dearest things—
Autumn leaves, or butterflies' wings!

And dandelions' fuzzy heads
They use to stuff their feather beds;

And yellow snapdragons supply
The nightcaps that the Fairies buy,

To which some blades of grass they pin,
And tie them 'neath each little chin.

Then, shopping done, the Fairies cry,
"Our Summer's gone! oh sweet, good-bye!"

And sadly to their caves they go,
To hide away from Winter's snow—

And then, though winds and storms may beat,
The Fairies' sleep is warm and sweet!

Margaret Deland.

Fable

The mountain and the squirrel
Had a quarrel,
And the former called the latter "Little Prig";
Bun replied:
"You are doubtless very big;
But all sorts of things and weather
Must be taken in together
To make up a year
And a sphere;
And I think it no disgrace
To occupy my place.
If I'm not so large as you,
You are not so small as I,
And not half so spry.
I'll not deny you make
A very pretty squirrel track;
Talents differ; all is well and wisely put;
If I cannot carry forests on my back
Neither can you crack a nut!"

Ralph Waldo Emerson.

THE POSY RING

A Midsummer Song

Oh, father's gone to market-town: he was up before the day,
And Jamie's after robins, and the man is making hay,
And whistling down the hollow goes the boy that minds the mill,
While mother from the kitchen-door is calling with a will,
"Polly!—Polly!—The cows are in the corn! Oh, where's Polly?"

From all the misty morning air there comes a summer sound,
A murmur as of waters, from skies and trees and ground.
The birds they sing upon the wing, the pigeons bill and coo;
And over hill and hollow rings again the loud halloo:
"Polly!—Polly!—The cows are in the corn! Oh, where's Polly?"

Above the trees, the honey-bees swarm by with buzz and boom,
And in the field and garden a thousand blossoms bloom.

Within the farmer's meadow a brown-eyed daisy blows,
And down at the edge of the hollow a red and thorny rose.
    But Polly!—Polly!—The cows are in the corn!
        Oh, where's Polly?

How strange at such a time of day the mill should stop its clatter!
The farmer's wife is listening now, and wonders what's the matter.
Oh, wild the birds are singing in the wood and on the hill,
While whistling up the hollow goes the boy that minds the mill.
    But Polly!—Polly!—The cows are in the corn!
        Oh, where's Polly!
            Richard Watson Gilder.

The Fairies of the Caldon-Low

"And where have you been, my Mary,
 And where have you been from me?"
"I've been to the top of the Caldon-Low,
 The midsummer night to see!"

"And what did you see, my Mary,
 All up on the Caldon-Low?"
"I saw the blithe sunshine come down,
 And I saw the merry winds blow."

"And what did you hear, my Mary,
 All up on the Caldon Hill?"
"I heard the drops of water made,
 And I heard the corn-ears fill."

"Oh, tell me all, my Mary—
 All, all that ever you know;
For you must have seen the fairies
 Last night on the Caldon-Low."

"Then take me on your knee, mother,
 And listen, mother of mine:
A hundred fairies danced last night,
 And the harpers they were nine;

"And merry was the glee of the harp-strings,
 And their dancing feet so small;

But oh! the sound of their talking
  Was merrier far than all!"

"And what were the words, my Mary,
  That you did hear them say?"
"I'll tell you all, my mother,
  But let me have my way.

"And some they played with the water
  And rolled it down the hill;
'And this,' they said, 'shall speedily turn
  The poor old miller's mill;

"'For there has been no water
  Ever since the first of May;
And a busy man shall the miller be
  By the dawning of the day!

"'Oh, the miller, how he will laugh,
  When he sees the mill-dam rise!
The jolly old miller, how he will laugh,
  Till the tears fill both his eyes!'

"And some they seized the little winds,
  That sounded over the hill,
And each put a horn into his mouth,
  And blew so sharp and shrill!

"'And there,' said they, 'the merry winds go,
  Away from every horn;

THE POSY RING

And those shall clear the mildew dank
  From the blind old widow's corn:

"'Oh, the poor blind widow—
  Though she has been blind so long,
She'll be merry enough when the mildew's gone,
  And the corn stands stiff and strong!'

" And some they brought the brown linseed,
  And flung it down from the Low:
'And this,' said they, ' by the sunrise,
  In the weaver's croft shall grow!

"'Oh, the poor lame weaver!
  How will he laugh outright
When he sees his dwindling flax-field
  All full of flowers by night!'

" And then upspoke a brownie,
  With a long beard on his chin;
' I have spun up all the tow,' said he,
  'And I want some more to spin.

"'I've spun a piece of hempen cloth,
  And I want to spin another—
A little sheet for Mary's bed
  And an apron for her mother.'

" And with that I could not help but laugh,
  And I laughed out loud and free;

And then on the top of the Caldon-Low,
  There was no one left but me.

" And all on the top of the Caldon-Low
  The mists were cold and gray,
And nothing I saw but the mossy stones
  That round about me lay.

" But, as I came down from the hill-top,
  I heard, afar below,
How busy the jolly old miller was,
  And how merry the wheel did go!

" And I peeped into the widow's field,
  And, sure enough, was seen
The yellow ears of the mildewed corn
  All standing stiff and green!

" And down by the weaver's croft I stole,
  To see if the flax were high;
But I saw the weaver at his gate
  With the good news in his eye!

" Now, this is all that I heard, mother,
  And all that I did see;
So, prithee, make my bed, mother,
  For I'm tired as I can be! "

Mary Howitt.

THE POSY RING

The Elf and the Dormouse

Under a toadstool
  Crept a wee Elf,
Out of the rain,
  To shelter himself.

Under the toadstool
  Sound asleep,
Sat a big Dormouse
  All in a heap.

Trembled the wee Elf,
  Frightened, and yet
Fearing to fly away
  Lest he get wet.

To the next shelter—
  Maybe a mile!
Sudden the wee Elf
  Smiled a wee smile,

Tugged till the toadstool
  Toppled in two.
Holding it over him,
  Gayly he flew.

Soon he was safe home,
  Dry as could be.

Soon woke the Dormouse—
  "Good gracious me!

"Where is my toadstool?"
  Loud he lamented.
—And that's how umbrellas
  First were invented.

Oliver Herford.

Meg Merrilies

Old Meg she was a gipsy,
  And lived upon the moors;
Her bed it was the brown heath turf,
  And her house was out of doors.
Her apples were swart blackberries,
  Her currants pods o' broom;
Her wine was dew of the wild white rose,
  Her book a churchyard tomb.

Her brothers were the craggy hills,
  Her sisters larchen-trees;
Alone with her great family
  She lived as she did please.
No breakfast had she many a morn,
  No dinner many a noon,
And 'stead of supper she would stare
  Full hard against the moon.

THE POSY RING

But every morn of woodbine fresh
   She made her garlanding,
And every night the dark glen yew
   She wore; and she would sing,
And with her fingers old and brown
   She plaited mats of rushes,
And gave them to the cottagers
   She met among the bushes.

Old Meg was brave as Margaret Queen,
   And tall as Amazon;
An old red blanket cloak she wore,
   A ship-hat had she on;
God rest her aged bones somewhere!
   She died full long agone!
                        John Keats.

Romance

I saw a ship a-sailing,
   A-sailing on the sea;
Her masts were of the shining gold,
   Her deck of ivory;
And sails of silk, as soft as milk,
   And silvern shrouds had she.

And round about her sailing,
   The sea was sparkling white,

The waves all clapped their hands and sang
  To see so fair a sight.
They kissed her twice, they kissed her thrice,
  And murmured with delight.

Then came the gallant captain,
  And stood upon the deck;
In velvet coat, and ruffles white,
  Without a spot or speck;
And diamond rings, and triple strings
  Of pearls around his neck.

And four-and-twenty sailors
  Were round him bowing low;
On every jacket three times three
  Gold buttons in a row;
And cutlasses down to their knees;
  They made a goodly show.

And then the ship went sailing,
  A-sailing o'er the sea;
She dived beyond the setting sun,
  But never back came she,
For she found the lands of the golden sands,
  Where the pearls and diamonds be.

Gabriel Setoun.

The Cow-Boy's Song

"Mooly cow, mooly cow, home from the wood
They sent me to fetch you as fast as I could.
The sun has gone down: it is time to go home.
Mooly cow, mooly cow, why don't you come?
Your udders are full, and the milkmaid is there,
And the children are waiting their supper to share.
I have let the long bars down,—why don't you pass through?"
 The mooly cow only said, "Moo-o-o!"

"Mooly cow, mooly cow, have you not been
Regaling all day where the pastures are green?
No doubt it was pleasant, dear mooly, to see
The clear running brook and the wide-spreading tree,
The clover to crop and the streamlet to wade,
To drink the cool water and lie in the shade;
But now it is night: they are waiting for you."
 The mooly cow only said, "Moo-o-o!"

"Mooly cow, mooly cow, where do you go,
When all the green pastures are covered with snow?
You go to the barn and we feed you with hay,
And the maid goes to milk you there, every day;

She speaks to you kindly and sits by your side,
She pats you, she loves you, she strokes your sleek hide:
Then come along home, pretty mooly cow, do."
   But the mooly cow only said, "Moo-o-o!"

"Mooly cow, mooly cow, whisking your tail,
The milkmaid is waiting, I say, with her pail;
She tucks up her petticoats, tidy and neat,
And places the three-leggéd stool for her seat:—
What can you be staring at, mooly? You know
That we ought to have gone home an hour ago.
How dark it is growing! O, what shall I do?"
   The mooly cow only said, "Moo-o-o!"

                                  Anna M. Wells.

IX
BED TIME

When the golden day is done,
  Through the closing portal,
Child and garden, flower and sun,
  Vanish all things mortal.
                Robert Louis Stevenson.

BED-TIME

Auld Daddy Darkness

Auld Daddy Darkness creeps frae his hole,
Black as a blackamoor, blin' as a mole:
Stir the fire till it lowes, let the bairnie sit,
Auld Daddy Darkness is no wantit yet.

See him in the corners hidin' frae the licht,
See him at the window gloomin' at the nicht;
Turn up the gas licht, close the shutters a',
An' Auld Daddy Darkness will flee far awa'.

Awa' to hide the birdie within its cosy nest,
Awa' to lap the wee flooers on their mither's breast,
Awa' to loosen Gaffer Toil frae his daily ca',
For Auld Daddy Darkness is kindly to a'.

He comes when we're weary to wean's frae oor waes,
He comes when the bairnies are getting aff their claes;
To cover them sae cosy, an' bring bonnie dreams,
So Auld Daddy Darkness is better than he seems.

Steek yer een, my wee tot, ye'll see Daddy then;
He's in below the bed claes, to cuddle ye he's fain;
Noo nestle in his bosie, sleep and dream yer fill,
Till Wee Davie Daylicht comes keekin' owre the hill.

      James Ferguson.

Wynken, Blynken, and Nod

Wynken, Blynken, and Nod one night
 Sailed off in a wooden shoe—
Sailed on a river of crystal light,
 Into a sea of dew.
"Where are you going, and what do you wish?"
 The old moon asked the three.
"We have come to fish for the herring fish
 That live in this beautiful sea;
 Nets of silver and gold have we!"
    Said Wynken,
    Blynken,
    And Nod.

The old moon laughed and sang a song,
 As they rocked in the wooden shoe,
And the wind that sped them all night long
 Ruffled the waves of dew.

The little stars were the herring fish
  That lived in that beautiful sea—
"Now cast your nets wherever you wish—
  Never afeard are we";
  So cried the stars to the fishermen three:
        Wynken,
        Blynken,
        And Nod.

All night long their nets they threw
  To the stars in the twinkling foam—
Then down from the skies came the wooden shoe,
  Bringing the fishermen home;
'Twas all so pretty a sail it seemed
  As if it could not be,
And some folks thought 'twas a dream they'd dreamed
  Of sailing that beautiful sea—
  But I shall name you the fishermen three:
        Wynken,
        Blynken,
        And Nod.

Wynken and Blynken are two little eyes,
  And Nod is a little head,
And the wooden shoe that sailed the skies
  Is a wee one's trundle-bed.

So shut your eyes while mother sings
   Of wonderful sights that be,
And you shall see the beautiful things
   As you rock in the misty sea,
      Where the old shoe rocked the fishermen three:
            Wynken,
            Blynken,
            And Nod.

Eugene Field.

Rockaby, Lullaby

Rockaby, lullaby, bees on the clover!—
Crooning so drowsily, crying so low—
Rockaby, lullaby, dear little rover!
   Down into wonderland—
   Down to the under-land—
      Go, oh go!
Down into wonderland go!

Rockaby, lullaby, rain on the clover!
Tears on the eyelids that struggle and weep!
Rockaby, lullaby—bending it over!
   Down on the mother world,
   Down on the other world!
      Sleep, oh sleep!
Down on the mother-world sleep!

Rockaby, lullaby, dew on the clover!
Dew on the eyes that will sparkle at dawn!
Rockaby, lullaby, dear little rover!
    Into the stilly world!
    Into the lily world,
        Gone! oh gone!
Into the lily world, gone!

                Josiah Gilbert Holland.

Sleep, My Treasure

  Sleep, sleep, my treasure,
  The long day's pleasure
Has tired the birds, to their nests they creep;
    The garden still is
    Alight with lilies,
But all the daisies are fast asleep.

  Sleep, sleep, my darling,
  Dawn wakes the starling,
The sparrow stirs when he sees day break;
    But all the meadow
    Is wrapped in shadow,
And you must sleep till the daisies wake!

                E. Nesbit.

Lullaby of an Infant Chief

Oh, hush thee, my babie, thy sire was a knight,
Thy mother a lady, both lovely and bright;
The woods and the glens from the tower which we see,
They all are belonging, dear babie, to thee.

Oh, fear not the bugle, though loudly it blows,
It calls but the warders that guard thy repose;
Their bows would be bended, their blades would be red,
Ere the step of a foeman draws near to thy bed.

Oh, hush thee, my babie, the time will soon come,
When thy sleep shall be broken by trumpet and drum;
Then hush thee, my darling, take rest while you may,
For strife comes with manhood, and waking with day.

Sir Walter Scott.

Sweet and Low

Sweet and low, sweet and low,
   Wind of the western sea,
Low, low, breathe and blow,
   Wind of the western sea!
Over the rolling waters go,
Come from the dying moon, and blow,
   Blow him again to me:
While my little one, while my pretty one, sleeps.

Sleep and rest, sleep and rest,
   Father will come to thee soon;
Rest, rest, on mother's breast,
   Father will come to thee soon;
Father will come to his babe in the nest,
Silver sails all out of the west
   Under the silver moon:
Sleep, my little one, sleep, my pretty one, sleep.

                      Alfred, Lord Tennyson.

Old Gaelic Lullaby

Hush! the waves are rolling in,
   White with foam, white with foam;
Father toils amid the din;
   But baby sleeps at home.

Hush! the winds roar hoarse and deep,—
   On they come, on they come!
Brother seeks the wandering sheep:
   But baby sleeps at home.

Hush! the rain sweeps o'er the knowes,
   Where they roam, where they roam;
Sister goes to seek the cows;
   But baby sleeps at home.

Unknown.

The Sandman

The rosy clouds float overhead,
   The sun is going down;
And now the sandman's gentle tread
   Comes stealing through the town.
"White sand, white sand," he softly cries,
   And as he shakes his hand,
Straightway there lies on babies' eyes
   His gift of shining sand.

THE POSY RING

Blue eyes, gray eyes, black eyes, and brown,
As shuts the rose, they softly close, when he goes
    through the town.

  From sunny beaches far away—
    Yes, in another land—
  He gathers up at break of day
    His store of shining sand.
  No tempests beat that shore remote,
    No ships may sail that way;
  His little boat alone may float
    Within that lovely bay.
Blue eyes, gray eyes, black eyes, and brown,
As shuts the rose, they softly close, when he goes
    through the town.

  He smiles to see the eyelids close
    Above the happy eyes;
  And every child right well he knows,—
    Oh, he is very wise!
  But if, as he goes through the land,
    A naughty baby cries,
  His other hand takes dull gray sand
    To close the wakeful eyes.
Blue eyes, gray eyes, black eyes, and brown,
As shuts the rose, they softly close, when he goes
    through the town.

So when you hear the sandman's song
   Sound through the twilight sweet,
Be sure you do not keep him long
   A-waiting on the street.
Lie softly down, dear little head,
   Rest quiet, busy hands,
Till, by your bed his good-night said,
   He strews the shining sands.
Blue eyes, gray eyes, black eyes, and brown,
As shuts the rose, they softly close, when he goes
     through the town.

                Margaret Vandegrift.

The Cottager to Her Infant

The days are cold, the nights are long,
The north-wind sings a doleful song;
Then hush again upon my breast;
All merry things are now at rest,
   Save thee, my pretty Love!

The kitten sleeps upon the hearth,
The crickets long have ceased their mirth;
There's nothing stirring in the house
Save one wee, hungry nibbling mouse,
   Then why so busy thou?

Nay ! start not at that sparkling light,
'Tis but the moon that shines so bright
On the window-pane bedropped with rain;
There, little darling ! sleep again,
   And wake when it is day.

                      Dorothy Wordsworth.

A Charm to Call Sleep

Sleep, Sleep, come to me, Sleep,
  Come to my blankets and come to my bed,
  Come to my legs and my arms and my head,
Over me, under me, into me creep.

Sleep, Sleep, come to me, Sleep,
  Blow on my face like a soft breath of air,
  Lay your cool hand on my forehead and hair,
Carry me down through the dream-waters deep.

Sleep, Sleep, come to me, Sleep,
  Tell me the secrets that you alone know,
  Show me the wonders none other can show,
Open the box where your treasures you keep.

Sleep, Sleep, come to me, Sleep :
  Softly I call you ; as soft and as slow
  Come to me, cuddle me, stay with me so,
Stay till the dawn is beginning to peep.

                      Henry Johnstone.

Night

The snow is white, the wind is cold—
The king has sent for my three-year-old.
Bring the pony and shoe him fast
With silver shoes that were made to last.
Bring the saddle trimmed with gold;
Put foot in stirrup, my three-year-old;
Jump in the saddle, away, away!
And hurry back by the break of day;
By break of day, through dale and down,
And bring me the news from Slumbertown.

                    Mary F. Butts.

Bed-Time

'Tis bed-time; say your hymn, and bid "Good night,
"God bless mamma, papa, and dear ones all."
Your half-shut eyes beneath your eye-lids fall;
Another minute you will shut them quite.
Yes, I will carry you, put out the light,
And tuck you up, although you are so tall.
What will you give me, Sleepy One, and call
My wages, if I settle you all right?
I laid her golden curls upon my arm,
I drew her little feet within my hand;

Her rosy palms were joined in trustful bliss,
Her heart next mine, beat gently, soft and warm;
She nestled to me, and, by Love's command,
Paid me my precious wages,—Baby's kiss.

       Lord Rosslyn.

Nightfall in Dordrecht

The mill goes toiling slowly around
 With steady and solemn creak,
And my little one hears in the kindly sound
 The voice of the old mill speak.
While round and round those big white wings
 Grimly and ghostlike creep,
My little one hears that the old mill sings:
 "Sleep, little tulip, sleep!"

The sails are reefed and the nets are drawn,
 And, over his pot of beer,
The fisher, against the morrow's dawn,
 Lustily maketh cheer;
He mocks at the winds that caper along
 From the far-off clamorous deep—
But we—we love their lullaby song
 Of "Sleep, little tulip, sleep!"

Old dog Fritz in slumber sound
   Groans of the stony mart—
To-morrow how proudly he'll trot you round,
   Hitched to our new milk-cart!
And you shall help me blanket the kine
   And fold the gentle sheep
And set the herring a-soak in brine—
   But now, little tulip, sleep!

A Dream-One comes to button the eyes
   That wearily droop and blink,
While the old mill buffets the frowning skies
   And scolds at the stars that wink;
Over your face the misty wings
   Of that beautiful Dream-One sweep,
And rocking your cradle she softly sings:
   "Sleep, little tulip, sleep!"

                         Eugene Field.

X

FOR SUNDAY'S CHILD

Sunday's child is full of grace.
Old Proverb.

FOR SUNDAY'S CHILD

All Things Bright and Beautiful

All things bright and beautiful,
    All creatures great and small,
All things wise and wonderful,
    The Lord God made them all.

Each little flower that opens,
    Each little bird that sings,
He made their glowing colours,
    He made their tiny wings.

The rich man in his castle,
    The poor man at his gate,
God made them, high or lowly,
    And order'd their estate.

The purple-headed mountain,
    The river running by,
The sunset and the morning,
    That brightens up the sky;—

The cold wind in the winter,
    The pleasant summer sun,

The ripe fruits in the garden,—
　　He made them every one;

The tall trees in the greenwood,
　　The meadows where we play,
The rushes by the water
　　We gather every day;—

He gave us eyes to see them,
　　And lips that we might tell,
How great is God Almighty,
　　Who has made all things well.
　　　　　　　　Cecil Frances Alexander.

The Still Small Voice

Wee Sandy in the corner
　　Sits greeting on a stool,
And sair the laddie rues
　　Playing truant frae the school;
Then ye'll learn frae silly Sandy,
　　Wha's gotten sic a fright,
To do naething through the day
　　That may gar ye greet at night.

He durstna venture hame now,
　　Nor play, though e'er so fine,

And ilka ane he met wi'
  He thought them sure to ken,
And started at ilk whin bush,
  Though it was braid daylight—
Sae do nothing through the day
  That may gar ye greet at night.

Wha winna be advised
  Are sure to rue ere lang;
And muckle pains it costs them
  To do the thing that's wrang,
When they wi' half the fash o't
  Might aye be in the right,
And do naething through the day
  That would gar them greet at night.

What fools are wilfu' bairns,
  Who misbehave frae hame!
There's something in the breast aye
  That tells them they're to blame;
And then when comes the gloamin',
  They're in a waefu' plight!
Sae do naething through the day
  That may gar ye greet at night.

Alexander Smart.

THE POSY RING

The Camel's Nose

Once in his shop a workman wrought,
With languid head and listless thought,
When, through the open window's space,
Behold, a camel thrust his face!
"My nose is cold," he meekly cried;
"Oh, let me warm it by thy side!"

Since no denial word was said,
In came the nose, in came the head:
As sure as sermon follows text,
The long and scraggy neck came next;
And then, as falls the threatening storm,
In leaped the whole ungainly form.

Aghast the owner gazed around,
And on the rude invader frowned,
Convinced, as closer still he pressed,
There was no room for such a guest;
Yet more astonished, heard him say,
"If thou art troubled, go away,
For in this place I choose to stay."

O youthful hearts to gladness born,
Treat not this Arab lore with scorn!
To evil habits' earliest wile
Lend neither ear, nor glance, nor smile.

Choke the dark fountain ere it flows,
Nor e'en admit the camel's nose!

     Lydia H. Sigourney.

A Child's Grace

Some hae meat and canna eat,
 And some wad eat that want it;
But we hae meat and we can eat,
 And sae the Lord be thankit.

     Robert Burns.

A Child's Thought of God

They say that God lives very high!
 But if you look above the pines
You cannot see our God. And why?

And if you dig down in the mines
 You never see Him in the gold,
Though from Him all that's glory shines.

God is so good, He wears a fold
 Of heaven and earth across His face—
Like secrets kept, for love, untold.

But still I feel that His embrace
 Slides down by thrills, through all things made,
Through sight and sound of every place:

As if my tender mother laid
  On my shut lids, her kisses' pressure,
Half-waking me at night; and said
  "Who kissed you through the dark, dear guesser?"

Elizabeth Barrett Browning.

The Lamb

Little lamb, who made thee?
Dost thou know who made thee,
Gave thee life and bade thee feed
By the stream and o'er the mead;
Gave thee clothing of delight,
Softest clothing, woolly, bright;
Gave thee such a tender voice,
Making all the vales rejoice?
Little lamb, who made thee?
Dost thou know who made thee?

Little lamb, I'll tell thee;
Little lamb, I'll tell thee.
He is callèd by thy name,
For He calls himself a Lamb.
He is meek and He is mild,
He became a little child.

I a child and thou a lamb,
We are callèd by His name.
Little lamb, God bless thee!
Little lamb, God bless thee!

     William Blake.

Night and Day

When I run about all day,
When I kneel at night to pray,
 God sees.

When I'm dreaming in the dark,
When I lie awake and hark,
 God sees.

Need I ever know a fear?
Night and day my Father's near:—
 God sees.

    Mary Mapes Dodge.

THE POSY RING

High and Low

The showers fall as softly
  Upon the lowly grass
As on the stately roses
  That tremble as they pass.

The sunlight shines as brightly
  On fern-leaves bent and torn
As on the golden harvest,
  The fields of waving corn.

The wild birds sing as sweetly
  To rugged, jagged pines,
As to the blossomed orchards,
  And to the cultured vines.

. . . . . .

Dora Read Goodale.

By Cool Siloam's Shady Rill

By cool Siloam's shady rill
  How sweet the lily grows!
How sweet the breath beneath the hill
  Of Sharon's dewy rose!

Lo, such the child whose early feet
  The paths of peace have trod;

Whose secret heart, with influence sweet,
  Is upward drawn to God.

. . . .

Reginald Heber.

Sheep and Lambs

All in the April morning,
  April airs were abroad;
The sheep with their little lambs
  Pass'd me by on the road.

The sheep with their little lambs
  Pass'd me by on the road;
All in an April evening
  I thought on the Lamb of God.

The lambs were weary, and crying
  With a weak human cry,
I thought on the Lamb of God
  Going meekly to die.

Up in the blue, blue mountains
  Dewy pastures are sweet:
Rest for the little bodies,
  Rest for the little feet.

. . . . . .

All in the April evening,
   April airs were abroad;
I saw the sheep with their lambs,
   And thought on the Lamb of God.
              Katharine Tynan Hinkson.

To His Saviour, a Child; A Present by a Child

Go, pretty child, and bear this flower
Unto thy little Saviour;
And tell him, by that bud now blown,
He is the Rose of Sharon known.
When thou hast said so, stick it there
Upon his bib or stomacher;
And tell him, for good hansel too,
That thou hast brought a whistle new,
Made of a clean strait oaten reed,
To charm his cries at time of need.
Tell him, for coral thou hast none,
But if thou hadst, he should have one;
But poor thou art, and known to be
Even as moneyless as he.
Lastly, if thou canst win a kiss
From those mellifluous lips of his;
Then never take a second on,
To spoil the first impression.
                    Robert Herrick.

What Would You See?

What would you see if I took you up
  To my little nest in the air?
You would see the sky like a clear blue cup
  Turned upside downwards there.

What would you do if I took you there
  To my little nest in the tree?
My child with cries would trouble the air,
  To get what she could but see.

What would you get in the top of the tree
  For all your crying and grief?
Not a star would you clutch of all you see—
  You could only gather a leaf.

But when you had lost your greedy grief,
  Content to see from afar,
You would find in your hand a withering leaf,
  In your heart a shining star.

                  George Macdonald.

Corn-Fields

When on the breath of Autumn's breeze,
   From pastures dry and brown,
Goes floating, like an idle thought,
   The fair, white thistle-down,—
Oh, then what joy to walk at will
Upon the golden harvest-hill!

What joy in dreaming ease to lie
   Amid a field new shorn;
And see all round, on sunlit slopes,
   The piled-up shocks of corn;
And send the fancy wandering o'er
All pleasant harvest-fields of yore!

I feel the day; I see the field;
   The quivering of the leaves;
And good old Jacob, and his horse,—
   Binding the yellow sheaves!
And at this very hour I seem
To be with Joseph in his dream!

I see the fields of Bethlehem,
   And reapers many a one
Bending unto their sickles' stroke,
   And Boaz looking on;
And Ruth, the Moabitess fair,
Among the gleaners stooping there!

THE POSY RING

Again, I see a little child,
   His mother's sole delight,—
God's living gift of love unto
   The kind, good Shunamite;
To mortal pangs I see him yield,
And the lad bear him from the field.

The sun-bathed quiet of the hills,
   The fields of Galilee,
That eighteen hundred years ago
   Were full of corn, I see;
And the dear Saviour take his way
'Mid ripe ears on the Sabbath-day.

Oh golden fields of bending corn,
   How beautiful they seem!
The reaper-folk, the piled-up sheaves,
   To me are like a dream;
The sunshine, and the very air
Seem of old time, and take me there!

                              Mary Howitt.

Little Christel

I

Slowly forth from the village church,—
  The voice of the choristers hushed overhead,—
Came little Christel. She paused in the porch,
  Pondering what the preacher had said.

Even the youngest, humblest child
  Something may do to please the Lord;
" Now, what," thought she, and half-sadly smiled,
  " Can I, so little and poor, afford ?—

" *Never, never a day should pass,*
  Without some kindness, kindly shown,
The preacher said "—Then down to the grass
  A skylark dropped, like a brown-winged stone.

" Well, a day is before me now ;
  Yet, what," thought she, " can I do, if I try ?
If an angel of God would show me how !
  But silly am I, and the hours they fly."

Then the lark sprang singing up from the sod,
  And the maiden thought, as he rose to the blue,
" He says he will carry my prayer to God ;
  But who would have thought the little lark knew ? "

THE POSY RING

II

Now she entered the village street,
  With book in hand and face demure,
And soon she came, with sober feet,
  To a crying babe at a cottage door.

It wept at a windmill that would not move,
  It puffed with round red cheeks in vain,
One sail stuck fast in a puzzling groove,
  And baby's breath could not stir it again.

So baby beat the sail and cried,
  While no one came from the cottage door;
But little Christel knelt down by its side,
  And set the windmill going once more.

Then babe was pleased, and the little girl
  Was glad when she heard it laugh and crow;
Thinking, " Happy windmill, that has but to whirl,
  To please the pretty young creature so."

III

No thought of herself was in her head,
  As she passed out at the end of the street,
And came to a rose-tree tall and red,
  Drooping and faint with the summer heat.

She ran to a brook that was flowing by,
  She made of her two hands a nice round cup,
And washed the roots of the rose-tree high,
  Till it lifted its languid blossoms up.

"O happy brook!" thought little Christel,
  "You have done some good this summer's day,
You have made the flowers look fresh and well!"
  Then she rose and went on her way.

. . . .

William Brighty Rands.

A Child's Prayer

God make my life a little light,
  Within the world to glow—
A tiny flame that burneth bright,
  Wherever I may go.

God make my life a little flower,
  That bringeth joy to all,
Content to bloom in native bower,
  Although its place be small.

God make my life a little song,
  That comforteth the sad,
That helpeth others to be strong,
  And makes the singer glad.

     M. Betham Edwards

XI

BELLS OF CHRISTMAS

*Then let the holly red be hung,
And all the sweetest carols sung,
While we with joy remember them—
The journeyers to Bethlehem.*
     Frank Dempster Sherman.

BELLS OF CHRISTMAS

The Adoration of the Wise Men

Saw you never in the twilight,
  When the sun had left the skies,
Up in heaven the clear stars shining,
  Through the gloom like silver eyes?
So of old the wise men watching,
  Saw a little stranger star,
And they knew the King was given,
  And they follow'd it from far.

Heard you never of the story,
  How they cross'd the desert wild,
Journey'd on by plain and mountain,
  Till they found the Holy Child?
How they open'd all their treasure,
  Kneeling to that Infant King,
Gave the gold and fragrant incense,
  Gave the myrrh in offering?

Know ye not that lowly Baby
  Was the bright and morning star,
He who came to light the Gentiles,
  And the darken'd isles afar?

And we too may seek his cradle,
  There our heart's best treasures bring,
Love, and Faith, and true devotion,
  For our Saviour, God, and King.

    Cecil Frances Alexander.

Cradle Hymn

Hush, my dear, lie still and slumber;
  Holy angels guard thy bed;
Heavenly blessings without number
  Gently falling on thy head.

Sleep, my babe, thy food and raiment,
  House and home, thy friends provide;
All without thy care, or payment,
  All thy wants are well supplied.

How much better thou'rt attended
  Than the Son of God could be,
When from heaven He descended,
  And became a child like thee!

Soft and easy is thy cradle;
  Coarse and hard thy Saviour lay,
When His birthplace was a stable,
  And His softest bed was hay.

THE POSY RING

See the kindly shepherds round him,
  Telling wonders from the sky!
When they sought Him, there they found Him,
  With his Virgin-Mother by.

See the lovely babe a-dressing;
  Lovely infant, how He smiled!
When He wept, the mother's blessing
  Soothed and hushed the holy child.

Lo, He slumbers in His manger,
  Where the honest oxen fed;
—Peace, my darling! here's no danger!
  Here's no ox a-near thy bed!

Mayst thou live to know and fear Him,
  Trust and love Him all thy days;
Then go dwell forever near Him,
  See His face, and sing His praise!

I could give thee thousand kisses,
  Hoping what I most desire;
Not a mother's fondest wishes
  Can to greater joys aspire.

Isaac Watts.

The Christmas Silence

Hushed are the pigeons cooing low
   On dusty rafters of the loft;
   And mild-eyed oxen, breathing soft,
Sleep on the fragrant hay below.

Dim shadows in the corner hide;
   The glimmering lantern's rays are shed
   Where one young lamb just lifts his head,
Then huddles 'gainst his mother's side.

Strange silence tingles in the air;
   Through the half-open door a bar
   Of light from one low-hanging star
Touches a baby's radiant hair.

No sound: the mother, kneeling, lays
   Her cheek against the little face.
   Oh human love! Oh heavenly grace!
'Tis yet in silence that she prays!

Ages of silence end to-night;
   Then to the long-expectant earth
   Glad angels come to greet His birth
In burst of music, love, and light!

                    Margaret Deland.

THE POSY RING

An Offertory

Oh, the beauty of the Christ Child,
　The gentleness, the grace,
　The smiling, loving tenderness,
　The infantile embrace!
　　All babyhood he holdeth,
　　All motherhood enfoldeth—
　Yet who hath seen his face?

Oh, the nearness of the Christ Child,
　When, for a sacred space,
　He nestles in our very homes—
　Light of the human race!
　　We know him and we love him,
　　No man to us need prove him—
　Yet who hath seen his face?

　　　　　　　　Mary Mapes Dodge.

Why Do Bells of Christmas Ring?

Why do the bells of Christmas ring?
Why do little children sing?

Once a lovely, shining star,
Seen by shepherds from afar,
Gently moved until its light
Made a manger's cradle bright.

There a darling baby lay,
Pillowed soft upon the hay;
And its mother sung and smiled,
"This is Christ, the holy child!"

Therefore bells for Christmas ring,
Therefore little children sing.

Eugene Field.

A Visit from St. Nicholas

'Twas the night before Christmas, when all through the house
Not a creature was stirring, not even a mouse.
The stockings were hung by the chimney with care,
In hopes that St. Nicholas soon would be there.
The children were nestled all snug in their beds,
While visions of sugar-plums danced in their heads;
And mamma in her kerchief, and I in my cap,
Had just settled our brains for a long winter's nap—
When out on the lawn there arose such a clatter
I sprang from my bed to see what was the matter.
Away to the window I flew like a flash,
Tore open the shutter, and threw up the sash.

THE POSY RING

The moon on the breast of the new-fallen snow
Gave a lustre of midday to objects below;
When what to my wondering eyes should appear
But a miniature sleigh and eight tiny reindeer,
With a little old driver, so lively and quick,
I knew in a moment it must be St. Nick!
More rapid than eagles his coursers they came,
And he whistled and shouted and called them by name.
"Now, Dasher! now, Dancer! now, Prancer and Vixen!
On, Comet! on, Cupid! on, Donder and Blitzen!—
To the top of the porch, to the top of the wall,
Now, dash away, dash away, dash away all!"
As dry leaves that before the wild hurricane fly,
When they meet with an obstacle mount to the sky,
So, up to the housetop the coursers they flew,
With a sleigh full of toys—and St. Nicholas, too.
And then, in a twinkling, I heard on the roof
The prancing and pawing of each little hoof.
As I drew in my head, and was turning around,
Down the chimney St. Nicholas came with a bound:
He was dressed all in fur from his head to his foot,
And his clothes were all tarnished with ashes and soot:

A bundle of toys he had flung on his back,
And he looked like a pedler just opening his pack.
His eyes, how they twinkled! his dimples, how merry!
His cheeks were like roses, his nose like a cherry;
His droll little mouth was drawn up like a bow,
And the beard on his chin was as white as the snow.
The stump of a pipe he held tight in his teeth,
And the smoke, it encircled his head like a wreath.
He had a broad face and a little round belly
That shook, when he laughed, like a bowl full of jelly.
He was chubby and plump—a right jolly old elf:
And I laughed when I saw him, in spite of myself;
A wink of his eye, and a twist of his head,
Soon gave me to know I had nothing to dread.
He spoke not a word, but went straight to his work,
And filled all the stockings: then turned with a jerk,
And laying his finger aside of his nose,
And giving a nod, up the chimney he rose.

THE POSY RING

He sprang to his sleigh, to his team gave a whistle,
And away they all flew like the down of a thistle.
But I heard him exclaim, ere they drove out of sight,
"Happy Christmas to all, and to all a good-night!"

Clement C. Moore.

The Christmas Trees

There's a stir among the trees,
There's a whisper in the breeze,
Little ice-points clash and clink,
Little needles nod and wink,
Sturdy fir-trees sway and sigh—
"Here am I! Here am I!"

"All the summer long I stood
In the silence of the woods.
Tall and tapering I grew;
What might happen well I knew;
For one day a little bird
Sang, and in the song I heard
Many things quite strange to me
Of Christmas and the Christmas tree.

"When the sun was hid from sight
In the darkness of the night,
When the wind with sudden fret
Pulled at my green coronet,
Staunch I stood, and hid my fears,
Weeping silent fragrant tears,
Praying still that I might be
Fitted for a Christmas tree.

"Now here we stand
On every hand!
In us a hoard of summer stored,
Birds have flown over us,
Blue sky has covered us,
Soft winds have sung to us,
Blossoms have flung to us
Measureless sweetness,
Now in completeness
We wait."

Mary F. Butts.

A Birthday Gift

. . . . . .

What can I give him,
Poor as I am?
If I were a shepherd
I would bring a lamb,
If I were a wise man
I would do my part,—
Yet what I can I give him,
    Give my heart.

                Christina Rossetti.

A Christmas Lullaby

Sleep, baby, sleep! The Mother sings:
Heaven's angels kneel and fold their wings.
        Sleep, baby, sleep!

With swathes of scented hay Thy bed
By Mary's hand at eve was spread.
        Sleep, baby, sleep!

At midnight came the shepherds, they
Whom seraphs wakened by the way.
        Sleep, baby, sleep!

And three kings from the East afar,
Ere dawn came, guided by the star.
>> Sleep, baby, sleep!

They brought Thee gifts of gold and gems,
Pure orient pearls, rich diadems.
>> Sleep, baby, sleep!

But Thou who liest slumbering there,
Art King of Kings, earth, ocean, air.
>> Sleep, baby, sleep!

Sleep, baby, sleep! The shepherds sing:
Through heaven, through earth, hosannas ring.
>> Sleep, baby, sleep!
>> John Addington Symonds.

I Saw Three Ships

I saw three ships come sailing in,
   On Christmas day, on Christmas day;
I saw three ships come sailing in,
   On Christmas day in the morning.

. . . .

Pray whither sailed those ships all three
   On Christmas day, on Christmas day?
Pray whither sailed those ships all three
   On Christmas day in the morning?

Oh, they sailed into Bethlehem
  On Christmas day, on Christmas day;
Oh, they sailed into Bethlehem
  On Christmas day in the morning.

And all the bells on earth shall ring
  On Christmas day, on Christmas day;
And all the bells on earth shall ring
  On Christmas day in the morning.

And all the angels in heaven shall sing
  On Christmas day, on Christmas day;
And all the angels in heaven shall sing
  On Christmas day in the morning.

And all the souls on earth shall sing
  On Christmas day, on Christmas day;
And all the souls on earth shall sing
  On Christmas day in the morning.

Old Carol.

Santa Claus

He comes in the night! He comes in the night!
  He softly, silently comes;
While the little brown heads on the pillows so white
  Are dreaming of bugles and drums.

He cuts through the snow like a ship through
    the foam,
  While the white flakes around him whirl;
Who tells him I know not, but he findeth the
    home
  Of each good little boy and girl.

His sleigh it is long, and deep, and wide;
  It will carry a host of things,
While dozens of drums hang over the side,
  With the sticks sticking under the strings.
And yet not the sound of a drum is heard,
  Not a bugle blast is blown,
As he mounts to the chimney-top like a bird,
  And drops to the hearth like a stone.

The little red stockings he silently fills,
  Till the stockings will hold no more;
The bright little sleds for the great snow hills
  Are quickly set down on the floor.
Then Santa Claus mounts to the roof like a
    bird,
  And glides to his seat in the sleigh;
Not the sound of a bugle or drum is heard
  As he noiselessly gallops away.

He rides to the East, and he rides to the West,
  Of his goodies he touches not one;

He eateth the crumbs of the Christmas feast
  When the dear little folks are done.
Old Santa Claus doeth all that he can;
  This beautiful mission is his;
Then, children, be good to the little old man,
  When you find who the little man is.

Unknown.

Neighbors of the Christ Night

Deep in the shelter of the cave,
  The ass with drooping head
Stood weary in the shadow, where
  His master's hand had led.
About the manger oxen lay,
  Bending a wide-eyed gaze
Upon the little new-born Babe,
  Half worship, half amaze.
High in the roof the doves were set,
  And cooed there, soft and mild,
Yet not so sweet as, in the hay,
  The Mother to her Child.
The gentle cows breathed fragrant breath
  To keep Babe Jesus warm,
While loud and clear, o'er hill and dale,
  The cocks crowed, "Christ is born!"

Out in the fields, beneath the stars,
   The young lambs sleeping lay,
And dreamed that in the manger slept
   Another, white as they.

———

These were Thy neighbors, Christmas Child;
   To Thee their love was given,
For in Thy baby face there shone
   The wonder-light of Heaven.

                  Nora Archibald Smith.

Cradle Hymn

Away in a manger, no crib for a bed,
The little Lord Jesus laid down his sweet head.
The stars in the bright sky looked down where
    he lay—
The little Lord Jesus asleep on the hay.

The cattle are lowing, the baby awakes,
But little Lord Jesus, no crying he makes.
I love thee, Lord Jesus! look down from the
    sky,
And stay by my cradle till morning is nigh.

                  Martin Luther.

The Christmas Holly

The holly! the holly! oh, twine it with bay—
  Come give the holly a song;
For it helps to drive stern winter away,
  With his garment so sombre and long;
It peeps through the trees with its berries of red,
  And its leaves of burnished green,
When the flowers and fruits have long been dead,
  And not even the daisy is seen.
Then sing to the holly, the Christmas holly,
  That hangs over peasant and king;
While we laugh and carouse 'neath its glittering boughs,
  To the Christmas holly we'll sing.
. . . .

Eliza Cook.

Said I to myself, here's a chance for me,
The Lilliput Laureate for to be!
And these are the Specimens I sent in
To Pinafore Palace.   Shall I win?
     William Brighty Rands.

INDEX

Adoration of the Wise Men, The, 257
All Things Bright and Beautiful, 237
Angel's Whisper, The, 139
Answer to a Child's Question, 62
Ant and the Cricket, The, 78
April, In, 8
Auld Daddy Darkness, 221

Baby Corn, 93
Baby Seed Song, 88
Beau's Reply, 112
Bed-Time, 232
Bells of Christmas, 255
Birdies with Broken Wings, 133
Birds in Spring, The, 54
Birds in Summer, 65
Bird's Song in Spring, 102
Birthday Gift, A, 267
Blessing for the Blessed, A, 129
Blind Boy, The, 160
Bluebird, The, 68
Blue Jay, The, 74
Boy and the Sheep, The 114
Boy, The, 128
Boy's Song, A, 165
Breeches, Going Into, 174
Bunch of Roses, A, 155
Butterflies, White, 78
By Cool Siloam's Shady Rill, 244

Camel's Nose, The, 240
Chanticleer, 72
Child, A Sleeping, 132
Child at Bethlehem, The, 155
Child's Fancy, A, 95
Child's Grace, A, 241

INDEX

Child's Laughter, A, 145
Child's Prayer, A, 252
Child's Thought of God, A, 241
Children, Little, 137
Children, Other Little, 123
Chill, A, 144
Christmas Holly, The, 273
Christmas Lullaby, A, 267
Christmas Silence, The, 260
Christmas Trees, The, 265
City Child, The, 173
Cleanliness, 126
Clouds, 40
Corn-Fields, 248
Cottager to Her Infant, 230
Cow-Boy's Song, The, 217
Cradle Hymn (Watts), 258
Cradle Hymn (Luther), 272

Daffy-Down-Dilly, 91
Daisy's Song, The, 103
Dandelions, 98
Day, A, 28
Deaf and Dumb, 159
Dear Little Violets, 101
Discontent, 193
Doll, Dressing the, 167
Doll, The Lost, 166
Dolladine, 167

Elf and the Dormouse, The, 213

Elf, The Little, 188

Fable, 206
Fairies of the Caldon-Low, The, 209
Fairies' Shopping, The, 204
Fairies, The Child and the, 187
Fairies, The Last Voyage of the, 184
Fairy Folk, The, 181
Fairy in Armor, A, 183
February, In, 5
Fern, A New, 186
Fern Song, 90
Flax Flower, The, 99
Flower Folk, The, 81
Fountain, The, 34

Garaine, Little, 140
Garden, In a, 151
Good Luck, For, 105
Good-Morning, 29
Good-Night and Good-Morning, 136
Grass, The Voice of the, 36
Guessing Song, 45

Hie Away, 176
High and Low, 244
How the Leaves Came Down, 17
Hunting Song, 176

INDEX

Infant Joy, 129
I Remember, I Remember, 135
I Saw Three Ships, 268

Jack Frost, 47

Kitten and Falling Leaves, The, 121

Lady Moon, 30
Lamb, The, 242
Lamb, The Pet, 116
Lambs in the Meadow, 115
Land of Story-Books, The, 172
Lark and the Rook, The, 56
Letter, A, to Lady Margaret Cavendish Holles-Harley, when a Child, 141
Little Christel, 250
Little Dandelion, 97
Little Gustava, 152
Little Land, The, 148
Little White Lily, 83
Lobster Quadrille, A, 202
Love and the Child, 142
Lucy Gray, 156
Lullaby of an Infant Chief, 226
Lullaby, Old Gaelic, 228

Magpie's Nest, The, 198
March, 6

Marjorie's Almanac, 3
May, 13
Meg Merrilies, 214
Midsummer Song, A, 207
Milking Time, 113
My Pony, 109

Nearly Ready, 7
Neighbors of the Christ Night, 271
Night, 232
Night and Day, 243
Nightfall in Dordrecht, 233
Nightingale and the Glow-worm, The, 195
Now the Noisy Winds Are Still, 33

Offertory, An, 261
O Lady Moon, 31
Old Gaelic Lullaby, 228
"One, Two, Three," 188
Owl, The, 70
Owl and the Pussy-Cat, The, 201

Pedlar's Caravan, The, 170
Piping Down the Valleys Wild, 131
Play-Time, 163
Polly, 143

Rain, Signs of, 41
Rivulet, The, 46

INDEX

Robert of Lincoln, 75
Robin Redbreast, 54
Robin Redbreast, An Epitaph on a, 67
Rockaby, Lullaby, 224
Romance, 215

St. Nicholas, A Visit from, 262
Sandman, The, 228
Santa Claus, 269
Sea-Song from the Shore, A, 171
Seal Lullaby, 113
September, 16
Seven Times One, 133
Sheep and Lambs, 245
Shower, A Sudden, 43
Singer, The, 73
Sleep, A Charm to Call, 231
Sleep, My Treasure, 225
Snowbird, The, 57
Snowdrops, 89
Snowflakes, 49
Song (Keats), 69
Song (Peacock), 104
Spaniel, On a, Called Beau, Killing a Young Bird, 111
Spring, 9
Spring and Summer, 14
Spring Song, 7
Spring, The Coming of, 11
Spring, The Voice of, 10

Storm, After the, 156
Strange Lands, 44
Summer Days, 15
Swallows, The, 53
Sweet and Low, 227

Thank You, Pretty Cow, 114
Thanksgiving Day, 196
Thanksgiving Fable, A, 197
The Water! the Water! 49
There's Nothing Like the Rose, 89
Thimble, What May Happen to a, 190
Titmouse, The, 64
To His Saviour, a Child; A Present by a Child, 246
Tree, The, 102

Violet Bank, A, 88
Violet, The, 90
Violets, 85
Voice, The Still Small, 238

Waterfall, The, 35
What Does Little Birdie Say? 69
What the Winds Bring, 29
What Would You See? 247
Where Go the Boats? 125
Who Stole the Bird's Nest? 59

INDEX

Why Do Bells of Christmas Ring? 261
Wild Geese, 71
Wild Winds, 32
Wind in a Frolic, The, 38
Wind, The, 33
Windy Nights, 31
Winter Night, 19

Wishing, 127
Wonderful World, The, 27
World's Music, The, 146
Wynken, Blynken, and Nod, 222

Year's Windfalls, A (Rossetti), 20
Young Dandelion, 86